STYLE AND SPLENDOUR

Style & Splendour

THE WARDROBE OF QUEEN MAUD OF NORWAY 1896–1938

ANNE KJELLBERG AND SUSAN NORTH
V&A PUBLICATIONS

First published by V&A Publications, 2005
V&A Publications
160 Brompton Road
London SW3 1HW

Distributed in North America by Harry N. Abrams, Inc.,
New York

The moral right of the author has been asserted.

All photographs of Queen Maud's wardrobe:
Teigens Fotoatelier AS

ISBN 1 85177 454 8

Library of Congress Control Number 2004111392

A catalogue record for this book is available
from the British Library.

Every effort has been made to seek permission to reproduce
those images whose copyright does not reside with the V&A,
and we are grateful to the individuals and institutions who
have assisted in this task. Any omissions are entirely un-
intentional, and the details should be addressed to V&A
Publications.

Designed by Area

Front jacket illustration: Evening dress 'Arlesienne', 1912–13
(see p. 82)
Back jacket illustration: Day dress 'Flirt', 1938–9 (see p. 84)
Frontispiece: Evening dress, 1906, by Morin-Blossier, Paris
(see p. 80)

Printed in Hong Kong.

Contents

Acknowledgements

As with all projects of this nature, *Style and Splendour*, involved the hard work and invaluable contributions of many people. The authors would like to thank Their Majesties King Harald and Queen Sonja of Norway for their support for this display and permission to use photographs in this first publication in English about Queen Maud's wardrobe.

We are indebted to John and Inger Fredriksen and Esther and Peter Smedvig for their generous donation in support of the display. We are most grateful to the Norwegian Ambassador Mr Tarald O. Brautaset and Mrs Elisabeth Mohr Brautaset for their exceptional efforts on behalf of the V&A and the National Museum of Art in Oslo in bringing *Style and Splendour* to fruition.

Many colleagues in Oslo made major contributions to *Style and Splendour*. In particular we are very grateful to Ann Ollestad, Director General, and Adviser Mette Michelsen of the Press, Cultural Relations and Information Department, Royal Norwegian Ministry of Foreign Affairs for the Ministry's generous financial support of the display in celebration of Norway's Centennial Anniversary. In addition, we would also like to thank Sune Nordgren, Director, and Martin Biehl, Head of Communications of the new National Museum in Oslo. Øyvind Stokke has been a key advocate of the project, first as Minister Counsellor for Press, Information and Cultural Affairs at the Royal Norwegian Embassy in London and then as Project Manager, Centennial Anniversary – Programme Abroad at the Royal Norwegian Ministry of Foreign Affairs in Oslo.

At the Royal Norwegian Embassy in London, John Petter Opdahl, Minister Counsellor for Press, Information and Cultural Affairs, and Hilde Chapman, Cultural Advisor, worked tirelessly in support of the display, and funded travel to Oslo and translation of the original publication, *Dronning Maud*, about Queen Maud's wardrobe.

We are very grateful to colleagues at our respective institutions for their hard work in making *Style and Splendour* happen. At the National Museum of Art/Decorative Arts and Design in Oslo, Museum Assistant Wenche Thiis-Evensen, Head of Exhibitions Vibeke Petersen and Textile Conservators Brit Kaupang, Sissel Myhrvold and Angela Musil-Jantjes provided invaluable help.

At the V&A, Nicole Newman's indefatigable assistance was essential to the success of *Style and Splendour*. Suzanne Lussier in FTF provided welcome assistance with this publication. Lynda Hillyer and her staff in Textile Conservation, and Sue Ridley and staff in Technical Services made the physical display of Queen Maud's clothes possible.

Many thanks to the Royal Palace and the Norsk Folkemuseum in Oslo for permission to reproduce photographs of Queen Maud. We are also grateful to the Royal Archives for use of their photograph, granted by permission of Her Majesty Queen Elizabeth II.

Introduction

The appeal of Queen Maud's wardrobe is immediate. Gleaming golden gowns, sharply tailored suits, beaded silk evening dresses – all of these speak of an era of style and splendour long since vanished. Who wore these beautiful garments, and for what occasions? From the photograph opposite she gazes back at us, dressed in an embroidered silk evening gown, reading her newspaper. And what of the trousered ski suit in this wardrobe? Could it have been worn by the same person? Let us follow this elegant woman and her exquisite clothing back through time to discover the history of fashion in the early twentieth century, along with the story of a royal lifestyle.

The period 1896 to 1938 covers enormous changes in fashionable dress for women, from the cumbersome and decorative clothing of the Victorian period, to the much lighter, simpler styles of dress of the Depression Era. Hemlines became shorter; for the first time in centuries, women exposed their legs. Trousers, once the exclusive preserve of men, could finally be worn by women following a world war and a long battle over sartorial propriety. The layers of underwear that encased women in the late nineteenth and early twentieth centuries were replaced by lightweight undergarments of man-made fabrics in the 1930s.

It is easy for us to document these radical changes by looking at photographs and surviving dress in museum collections, but it is more difficult to imagine this evolution occurring within the span of one woman's lifetime. While we know millions of women underwent these transitions, there exist few collections of surviving dress covering this period of time, identified with a particular person, that illustrate these modifications so clearly.

Not only does Queen Maud's wardrobe allow us to record startling changes in fashion; it also chronicles her particular taste in clothes in interaction with the sartorial etiquette of the period. As a daughter of Edward VII, and by virtue of her role as Queen of Norway, Maud had many conventions and regulations of dress to consider and follow for all of her public appearances. But she was also a sister,

wife, mother, grandmother and private person who, as her wardrobe indicates, could dress as she pleased when out of the limelight.

This is also a political story chronicling Norway's independence, which was peacefully attained in 1905, and Maud's sudden and unexpected elevation to queen. As her role in life and homeland dramatically changed, so did her wardrobe. It is most fitting that Queen Maud's wardrobe should return briefly for display in the country of her birth in 2005, in celebration of the one-hundredth anniversary of Norway's independence.

This generous loan from the National Museum of Art/Museum of Decorative Arts and Design in Oslo is just a fraction of the magnificent collection of clothing left by Queen Maud and preserved at the royal palace in Oslo after her death. In 1961, her son King Olav donated a representative selection of her wardrobe to the Kunstindustrimuseet (Museum of Decorative Art, now the National Museum of Art/Museum of Decorative Arts and Design) in Oslo. Some thirty years later, her grandson King Harald, Princess Ragnhild (Mrs Lorentzen) and Princess Astrid (Mrs Ferner) gave the rest of Queen Maud's clothing to the museum.[1] The royal family's impressive gift is extensive. It contains examples of the magnificent outfits worn by Queen Maud for grand occasions both at home and abroad during a period of forty years, as well as clothing worn for more informal events and private pursuits. In addition, the gift includes shoes, hats, gloves, shawls and other accessories, primarily from the 1930s. The variety of garments, the time span they cover, their high quality and the extensive range of accessories make Queen Maud of Norway's wardrobe unique among the dress collections in the world's museums.

Additional documentation has filled in the stories behind Queen Maud's clothes. A few outfits arrived at the museum with information about the occasions for which they had been used and who had made them. Further research by the curator of Queen Maud's collection, Anne Kjellberg, has added much detail concerning the fashion houses that made

Photo of
Queen Maud in a
Laferrière evening
gown, 1909
Anderson/Det
Kongelige Slott,
Oslo

the garments, the events for which they were worn and the background of contemporary fashion against which they stand. Another very important source is a book in which the queen's dressers (personal maids devoted to the care of the queen's wardrobe and helping her dress each day) noted down which outfits Queen Maud wore on different important occasions from 1919 to 1938, which helps to link the clothes to makers and events.

The words of Queen Maud herself also provide a great insight into her taste and the sartorial demands her wardrobe served. Her letters to her sister-in-law Queen Mary, now in the Royal Archives in Windsor Castle, give glimpses of her life and thoughts during a period of more than forty years. Maud was a bridesmaid at the wedding of Princess May (as Queen Mary was known) in 1893 and they corresponded regularly with family news over the following decades. From a fashion perspective, the two form an interesting contrast. Queen Mary's sartorial style never evolved past 1914. At the behest of her husband George V, she retained her ankle-length skirts and cloche hats until her death in 1953.[2] Queen Maud, on the other hand, engaged with contemporary fashion throughout her life, balancing the conservatism of her royal role with her knowledge of what suited her best and her love of fashionable dress.

Queen Maud of Norway
1869–1938

Maud Charlotte Mary Victoria was born at Marlborough House in London on 26 November 1869, daughter of Edward Albert, the Prince of Wales, and Alexandra, Princess of Wales, and granddaughter of Queen Victoria. She was the fifth child of the Prince and Princess of Wales, having two older brothers, Prince Albert Victor and Prince George, and two older sisters, Princess Louise and Princess Victoria. Princess Alexandra was renowned for her style and taste in clothing. Naturally slender, with a taste for simplicity in her dress, Alexandra served as Britain's royal fashion icon at a time when Queen Victoria had long since retreated into widowhood.[1]

Princess Maud and her siblings were brought up mainly at the family estate at Sandringham in Norfolk, in a frugal but relaxed atmosphere. Princess Alexandra participated in a variety of sports, including riding, skating and yachting, in which her children took part. They also spent time with their mother's Danish family, one of whom was Prince Carl,

Maud's cousin and future husband. Carl, who was called Charles by his English relatives, was born on 3 August 1872. He was the son of Princess Alexandra's brother Crown Prince Frederik, later King Frederik VIII of Denmark, and his wife Louise, who was a Swedish-Norwegian princess by birth.[2]

On 28 October 1895, Princess Maud's engagement to Prince Carl of Denmark was announced. She was twenty-five years old; he had just turned twenty-three and was training as a naval officer. The engagement appears to have been a love match, and an item in Maud's wardrobe seems to confirm this. 'To be kept always…' was written on the outside of a parcel enclosing a lilac blouse with white polka dots from the mid-1890s, suggesting that it might have been the blouse Maud was wearing when Carl proposed to her.

Blessed with her mother's slender figure, Princess Maud had a regular, oval face with a small mouth and a long, slender nose. Her eyes were greenish in hue and delineated

The Prince and Princess of Wales with their daughters, Princess Maud in the centre, 1883
Det Kongelige Slott, Oslo

with clearly defined eyebrows. Her hair was light brown with a hint of reddish gold. Princess Maud's youth and attractiveness meant that her engagement generated considerable press attention. Several periodicals issued special wedding supplements with information about the bride and groom, their families, the wedding, the gifts and the bride's trousseau.

Princess Maud was married on 22 July 1896 in the chapel of Buckingham Palace. She wore an ivory silk satin and white chiffon dress with a belt of silver embroidery and artificial diamonds. Her wedding gown was designed by Rosalie Whyte, a student of the Royal Female School of Art, and made by Mmes Berthé and Yeo of London.[3] Maud wore her mother's veil of handmade Honiton lace, with a headdress of orange blossom. Unfortunately, Princess Maud's wedding dress has not survived, but her going-away dress, a cape and a walking suit from her trousseau, are the earliest items in her wardrobe (pages 97, 92 and 94).

In December 1896, Princess Maud left for her new home in the Bernstorff Mansion in Copenhagen. She and Prince Carl led a simple life; he was an officer in the Royal Danish Navy and was often away at sea. Frequent visits to Britain kept Maud in touch with her close-knit family, and she participated in the 1897 Jubilee and her father's coronation in 1902. The following year, Princess Maud gave birth to a son, who was christened Alexander Edward Christian Frederik. However, this quiet life was soon transformed by events that were happening outside both Britain and Denmark.

Princess Maud (right) in her wedding dress with her sister Princess Victoria, 22 July 1896
Det Kongelige Slott, Oslo

Norway had been in political union with Sweden for ninety years, but the Norwegians were increasingly unhappy with the arrangement. On 7 June 1905, as a result of a constitutional disagreement, Norway declared the union dissolved. Sweden requested a referendum on the issue and in August 1905, 368,392 Norwegians voted to end the union; there were only 184 votes against it.[4] Faced with such overwhelming agreement on the dissolution of the union, Sweden conceded. The form of government Norway should adopt then needed to be decided. In a referendum, a large majority of the Norwegian population voted in favour of a monarchy rather than a republic, and on 18 November 1905 the Storting, Norway's parliamentary assembly, chose the Danish Prince Carl to be King of Norway. Carl changed his name to Haakon upon election, and his son Alexander became Crown Prince Olav. Princess Maud was now Queen of Norway.

The new Norwegian royal family arrived in Kristiania (renamed Oslo in 1925) on 25 November 1905 and spent the next six months preparing for their coronation. King Haakon and Queen Maud were crowned on 22 June 1906 in Nidaros Cathedral in Trondhjem. At the age of thirty-six, Maud's life changed completely. Although raised as a princess, she quickly realized that being a queen in Norway was very different from being one in Britain or Denmark. Norway had no nobility to create a social circle around the

11

The Norwegian Royal Family: Queen Maud, Crown Prince Olav and King Haakon, 1907
Det Kongelige Slott, Oslo

informal socially, the Norwegians soon created a government that was far more progressive and liberal than most governments in Europe. King Haakon and Queen Maud worked hard to fit into their homeland and adapt to a nation that was reinventing itself day by day.

Queen Maud's life was now full of official events and ceremonies, including state visits abroad, and her wardrobe reflects this public side of her life in a wide range of evening gowns and formal daywear. She spent a few months of every year at Appleton House, her residence on the Sandringham estate in Britain. Over the next thirty years, she participated in a number of British royal events, including the Silver Jubilee of her brother George V in 1935, and the coronation of her nephew George VI in 1937. Her wardrobe also indicates that she found time for herself and her family, and that she continued the pursuit of a variety of sports that had begun in her childhood.

Queen Maud's life and work came to an end in the late autumn of 1938. During a stay in Britain, she was admitted to hospital in London for an operation and King Haakon immediately left Oslo to be with her. She died a few days later on 20 November. Queen Maud was brought home aboard the English battleship the *Royal Oak*. The ship arrived in Oslo on 26 November, the date of her sixty-ninth birthday. Her funeral was held in Oslo Cathedral on 8 December and she was buried in the Royal Mausoleum at Akershus Castle, having been Queen of Norway for thirty-three years.

court. Many Norwegians worried that the new royal court would pay too much attention to external splendour and prove expensive to run. Society and government in Norway were very different from those in Britain. Relaxed and

Royal Robes

'Behold! I am a Queen!!! Who w[oul]d have thought it?
& I am the very last person to be stuck on a throne!'[1]

This amusing comment came from Maud on 17 December 1905, just three weeks after her arrival in Norway and only a month after the invitation from the Norwegian parliament to Prince Carl. As Princess Maud, she had attended the coronation of her father Edward VII in 1902, but being the one to be crowned was quite a different prospect. There is no doubt that Queen Maud's coronation in 1906 was the most solemn occasion of her life, and its preparation caused her some concern. 'It *all* haunts *me* like an *awful* nightmare this Coronation & that it is *just* to be *ours* of *all* people!'[2] One of her greatest worries was appropriate clothing.

All coronations require spectacular dresses and royal robes. Norway had not had its own monarch since the fourteenth century, although coronations of Norwegian-Swedish kings and queens were held in Trondhjem, Norway in the 1800s. King Haakon and Queen Maud used the royal robes and regalia made for these coronations. As a new arrival in the country, Maud was very eager to be accepted and to be seen to be correctly and elegantly dressed. The creation of

her coronation gown was a special collaboration between Silkehuset, a fashion house in Kristiania (Oslo), and Vernon, a London court dressmaker.

For her father's coronation and that of her nephew George VI in 1937, Queen Maud relied on two of the fashion houses she regularly patronized for special gowns: something in keeping with contemporary fashion, but made with lavish materials and a long train to suit the occasion. Ede & Ravenscroft, the specialist robe makers in Britain, provided the purple velvet robe (a cape with a very long train), trimmed with ermine as decreed by the regulations governing coronations in Britain.

While the first two coronations Maud attended may have caused her some worry, she took the last one, in 1937, very much in her stride, writing afterwards to Queen Mary: 'It *all* seems like a dream now those *wonderful* unforgettable days, ... Can't get over *how* beautifully dear Bertie & Elizabeth did it *all* at the Coronation, *so* dignified & calm & *so* charming to *every* one.'[3]

Princess Maud's dress for the coronation of Edward VII, 1902

LAFERRIÈRE, PARIS

The National Museum of Art/
Museum of Decorative Arts and Design, Oslo
OK 3-1962

14 This gown from Queen Maud's wardrobe is probably the one she wore for her father's coronation on 9 August 1902. It resembles most closely the gown she is seen wearing in illustrations and photographs of the event. However, the sleeves appear to have been altered at least twice. A photograph of Queen Maud wearing this dress in 1905 shows a pair of sleeves made of a coarser lace. Maud frequently remade and altered her clothing and this economy extended even to royal gowns.

The dress was made by the Paris fashion house Laferrière. It has a machine-lace overdress in the princess style, richly embroidered with gilt metal thread. Diamanté and silver sequins emphasize the floral motif of the lace and enhance the shimmering effect of the gown. Only the grandest of occasions required such a long train.

Laferrière was a leading name in Paris fashion between 1880 and 1910, listed in Baedeker's *Guide to Paris* 1890–1 along with couturiers Worth and Pingat. At the World Exhibition in Paris in 1900, Laferrière exhibited with Worth, Callot Soeurs, Doeuillet, Paquin, Redfern and Rouff. The company was reputed to have started in 1847, but no trace of it has been found so early.[4] Laferrière may have begun by making luxury underwear, which was its speciality around the 1870s.[5] Three of Queen Maud's most splendid gala and evening gowns worn during her first years in Norway came from Laferrière. Designs by Laferrière continued to appear in French fashion magazines until about 1915, although the company seems to have ceased trading shortly after this time.[6]

Queen Maud of Norway's coronation dress, 1906

VERNON OF LONDON AND SILKEHUSET
OF KRISTIANIA (OSLO)

The National Museum of Art/
Museum of Decorative Arts and Design, Oslo
OK 1-1962

The coronation of King Haakon and Queen Maud took place on 22 June 1906 in Nidaros Cathedral in Trondhjem. Queen Maud's coronation dress was made of gold lamé in the princess style with scalloped lace sleeves. Its decorative pattern of flowers and ribbon bows is embroidered in gilt metal thread, gold-coloured sequins, artificial pearls and diamanté. The flowing expanse of golden fabric so richly embellished fully befits a queen.

The dress is probably a joint order between Vernon, the London fashion house, and Silkehuset of Kristiania. It is not clear how they worked together. Inside the belt of the dress is a label marked Vernon, while a sample of the embroidery for it was on display for many years at Silkehuset and was

described as their 'pride and joy'.[7] This corresponds with the story printed in the British press in 1906, that the dress was sewn in London, but that it was wholly or partially embroidered in Norway.[8] However, the Norwegian press told another version, namely that Silkehuset had both sewn the dress from material specially woven in Lyons, and made a sample of the embroidery that was carried out by a well-known fashion house in Paris.[9] If the Norwegian press was correct, Queen Maud must have ordered the dress at Silkehuset, but sent it to Vernon after it was completed for the final alterations. If so, then Vernon put its label in the garment even though it was not completely responsible for it. The exact sequence of construction may never been known, but the gown appropriately represents a collaboration of dressmakers from Queen Maud's country of birth and her new homeland.

The coronation of
King Haakon and
Queen Maud,
Cathedral of
Trondhjem,
22 June 1906
Wilse/Norsk
Folkemuseum, Oslo

Queen Maud's gown and robe for the coronation of King George VI, 1937

GOWN POSSIBLY BY WORTH, LONDON AND ROBE BY EDE AND RAVENSCROFT, LONDON

The National Museum of Art/
Museum of Decorative Arts and Design, Oslo
OK 19-1962 and OK 32-1962

The dress worn by Queen Maud at the coronation of her nephew George in 1937 is made from gold lamé tinged with pale pink. The slight hint of pink is reinforced by elbow-length sleeves of pink chiffon, embroidered with golden beads and edged in gold fringing. The bias-cut skirt starts from a point at the front of the bodice and ends in a long train at the back.

According to the notes of Queen Maud's dressers, she wore a gold dress by Worth for a dinner a Buckingham Palace on 10 May and a gold dress is also recorded for the coronation. The assumption is that these notes refer to the same dress.

For the coronation ceremony Queen Maud used the ermine-trimmed purple velvet robe she wore for her father's coronation in 1902. It was made by Ede and Ravenscroft, a company founded in 1689 and still in business today as specialists in ceremonial attire. For the coronation of Edward VII, Ede and Ravenscroft made the coronation

robes and the robes for members of the royal family, as well as ceremonial suits for the nobility, the court and the clergy.[10]

In the accounts of Ede and Ravenscroft, the details and the price of Princess Maud's robe are entered on 24 June 1902 under the title H.R.H. Princess Charles of Denmark. The title was later amended to H.M. Queen of Norway. The purple velvet robe trimmed with gold lace and ermine, and lined with white silk, cost 96 guineas. Included in the bill was red velvet for Maud's princess crown at 15 shillings, as well as a lacquered lead box in which to store the gown with Maud's name painted on it in gold, costing two pounds, seven shillings and sixpence.[11]

Dressed in her golden gown, ermine-edged robe, necklaces and diamond tiara, as well as her medals, Maud embodied British royal tradition, for she took part in the ceremony as a British princess, not as a Norwegian queen. Her husband King Haakon did not accompany her, as British coronation etiquette did not allow the kings of other countries to participate.

19

King George VI and Queen Elizabeth with their daughters and the King's closest relatives on their coronation day, Queen Maud on the far right, 12 May 1937
Hay Wrightson/Det Kongelige Slott, Oslo

Evening Dresses

'And the Queen! Yes, she was radiant, just like a Queen of Fairy Tales,…'[1]

So wrote the Norwegian ladies' magazine *Urd* on 9 December 1905, after King Haakon and Queen Maud had attended their first civic ball upon arriving in Norway to take up their new royal duties. For Maud, this meant a much more demanding personal role. Naturally shy, she found being in the limelight uncomfortable. Although she had been brought up as a princess, her childhood had been sheltered and early married life fairly quiet and undemanding. Now Maud was a queen, however, she had to live up to the expectations of her public and ensure that her clothes looked perfect for all her appearances.

The great range of evening dresses in Queen Maud's wardrobe from the period 1910 to 1938 are testimony to the many formal events in which she participated. Viewed chronologically, they document the changes in fashion through these three decades and to what degree Queen Maud took up new styles. Some fashions were too extreme or too casual for her lifestyle; others did not appeal to her personal taste. In most instances, she would not be the first to wear the latest fashion, and she always adapted it to her own preferences in dress. She was petite in stature and therefore chose styles that emphasized the vertical and made her appear taller. She was also very slender and proud of her tiny waist, which on some of her gowns measured only 46 cm (18 inches), and selected designs that accentuated these features.[2] Nevertheless, she embraced all the evolutions in fashion, from the high-waisted Directoire style initiated by the French designer Paul Poiret, through the low- or no-waisted look of the 1920s, to the elongated, classically inspired fashions of the 1930s.

Both in Norway and abroad, Queen Maud was renowned during her life for her beautiful clothes and stylish taste. Shortly after her coronation, the Norwegian newspaper *Morgenbladet* reported that 'the style and exquisite distinction of her toilettes always seem attractive to aesthetic taste'.[3] A far more difficult audience to please was the French press, but even here, Maud made a considerable impression. In 1907, the French journal *Femina* commented, 'Queen Maud has a stunning appearance. But is she not the daughter of Queen Alexandra of England who is famous for her grace and elegance?'[4]

Although Queen Maud sometimes found formal occasions trying, they did give her the opportunity to do something she loved, and that was to dance, an activity that also provided her with the chance to meet a variety of her subjects, as she explains: 'Our two big balls were a great success & everyone danced tremendously, I danced to *every* dance, & the officers really dance very well & then I get to know different people like that'[5]

Three evening gowns, 1907–9

CENTRE GOWN BY LAFERRIÈRE, PARIS

The National Museum of Art/
Museum of Decorative Arts and Design, Oslo
OK 6-1962, OK 13-1962, OK 4-1962

22   Three evening dresses from Queen Maud's wardrobe illustrate the splendour of formal wear at the end of the first decade of the twentieth century. On the left is a gown of rose pink silk. The elaborate trimmings of the bodice and hem contrast with the expanse of unadorned silk. The bodice is decorated with lace embroidered in silk and metal thread, glass beads and diamanté, while ruches of tulle and applied silk flowers edge the skirt.

On the right is a dress of pale yellow silk, with an overdress of tulle embroidered with a variety of golden beads and sequins. The embroidery is worked so that the dress appears to consist of two parts: a skirt and an overdress that is short at the front and ends in a square train at the back. The narrow, vertical pattern of the embroidery emphasizes the elongated style of the dress, as do the tight, elbow-length sleeves.

The ice-green silk dress in the centre was made by Laferrière and is embroidered in green and silver. The dress is shaped like a pinafore over a blouse of metal lace, and the right front drapes asymmetrically over the left. Queen Maud wears this dress in a photograph taken in 1909, reproduced on page 9.

These dresses demonstrate developments in fashion and Maud's particular preferences for her clothes. The princess style was widely worn in 1906, and the periodical *The Lady's Realm* wrote that this shape was the most elegant style for wedding and evening gowns.[6] Maud's choice of dresses in the princess style was probably a conscious one on her part, as it flattered her petite frame. A far more radical change was under way at this time in the form of Paul Poiret's Directoire style, based on the simple, high-waisted style of dress worn between 1795 and 1815. Although none of these three gowns has a waist seam, it is clear that the waistline – the narrowest width of the gown – has risen slightly above its natural level.

Evening dress, 1910–13

The National Museum of Art/
Museum of Decorative Arts and Design, Oslo
OK 14-1962

By 1910, Maud had embraced the new, high-waisted fashion, and this is a particularly beautiful example of the Directoire style. Made of white silk, the dress is embroidered with silk and glass beads in a meandering pattern of leaves and medallion-like flowers encircling birds, in black, white and silver. The dress presents a slim silhouette, with short bodice and a slender skirt extending into a long train. A narrow strip of black tulle winds around the dress from the waist, down the edge of the skirt and up again, accentuating the vertical line. Asymmetrical draping and the spidery, curvilinear lines of the floral embroidery are reminiscent of the Art Nouveau style that was popular at the time. The combination of white and black may indicate that Queen Maud wore it while in mourning for the death of her father Edward VII, who died on 6 May 1910.

Evening gown, 1912–13

The National Museum of Art/
Museum of Decorative Arts and Design, Oslo
OK 200-1991

Another example of Maud's variation of the Directoire style can be seen in this evening gown beaded in a pattern of stylized flowers with shades of mauve and white. The high-waisted gown is draped asymmetrically and held with a plastic clasp decorated with diamanté. Another clasp closes the gown at about knee level, allowing it to fall in folds and giving a glimpse of the undergown. Such draped details are typical of the styles of 1912 and 1913. In addition, this gown features loose, asymmetrical sleeves rather than the short, tight sleeves that appear on Maud's earlier gowns. These were also fashionable for the period and reflect the influence of designers such as Poiret, whose garments embodied fabrics that were loosely cut and allowed to drape over the figure.

25

Two evening gowns, 1910–13

The National Museum of Art/
Museum of Decorative Arts and Design, Oslo
OK 11-1962, OK 7-1962

While Paul Poiret's Directoire style may have simplified the cut of women's dresses when it was introduced in 1906, variations and complications in his elegant vertical lines soon developed. Designs for daywear favoured unadorned fabrics, but the formal demands of evening dress meant that sumptuous, richly embellished materials remained fashionable.

The blue dress has a skirt of satin, which is caught up in front over a beaded tunic. Layers of lace and embroidered chiffon form the upper part of the bodice. The hems of the gown and train are trimmed with fur, and more lace can be seen where the satin is pulled up in front.

The red dress is made of a variety of materials, creating layers of contrast, including pink silk, silver lace, red silk chiffon with silver embroidery and diamanté, as well as deep red velvet. The velvet fills in the neckline, circles the high waist with a bow at the front and forms a band at knee height with a bow at the back.

The strong colours of these dresses were not only to Maud's taste, but also typical of the fashions of 1910 to 1920. They reflect the influence of the costumes of the Ballets Russes, whose vibrant hues banished the pastels of the Edwardian period. Hemlines for daywear rose above the ankle for the first time in centuries, although for evening gowns a longer skirt was still essential. Maud's evening dresses, although still floor length, have short trains or none at all.

Two sequinned evening gowns, 1918-20

The National Museum of Art/
Museum of Decorative Arts and Design, Oslo
OK 205-1991, OK 206-1991

28 It is tempting to think that these two stunning, black-sequinned gowns were inspired by the northern lights so visible in Maud's new homeland. The streams of light swirling from a star-like shape on the dress on the right are reminiscent of Vincent Van Gogh's famous work *Starry, Starry Night*, painted in 1889. Heavily sequinned gowns had been fashionable for decades, but the abstract nature of the patterns of these two examples, the stark contrasts of colour and their very simple shapes are completely modern and representative of the twentieth century. In addition, the short length of the dress on the left must have exposed Maud's ankle after 6 p.m. for the first time in her life.

The severe and economical cut of these dresses may reflect the shortages of luxury goods in Europe during the First World War and the virtue fashion made of the situation. Several of Queen Maud's evening dresses from between 1918 and 1920 are of a similar style, with floating lines that follow the curves of the body without fitting closely. The dresses no longer have boning in the bodice, and the waistline, although still high, is rarely marked in any way other than through the decoration.

The dress on the left has beaded and diamanté borders, with silver sequins and glass beads at the bottom of the skirt and on the square train, along the horizontal neckline and on the double shoulder straps. The rows of sequins run in a variety of directions, reflecting the light from different angles and creating a dazzling sparkle on the black surface.

Queen Maud could have worn this black dress at one of the occasions she mentioned in a letter of 18 February 1920, in which she refers to another icon of the twentieth century: 'We gave a rather successful dance on the 2nd for *70* people & had an amusing band of mandolins & guitars *wh*[ich] was pretty & they played *all* the delightful new tunes *wh*[ich] I have on my gramophone.'[7]

Evening dress, *c.*1920

The National Museum of Art/
Museum of Decorative Arts and Design, Oslo
OK 15-1962

30 This gown of pink chiffon, with a pink and silver brocade tabard and Medici collar, may have been influenced by the designs of Mariano Fortuny, in style if not in colour. His simple, pleated silk 'Delphos' dresses, first made in 1907, would probably have been too radically artistic for Queen Maud – and indeed, her lifestyle had no need for such bohemian styles. However, Fortuny drew influence from a wide range of cultures and periods, including the Renaissance. He made a number of tabard dresses with long, rectangular panels of printed velvets extending from the front hem over the shoulders into a short train at the back, similar to this example. Like most designers whose creations originate completely outside contemporary fashion, Fortuny's were eventually absorbed into mainstream dress design. It is highly unlikely that Queen Maud ever owned a Fortuny, but whoever made this evocatively medieval dress for her must have been familiar with his designs.

Detail of evening cape, 1920

The National Museum of Art/
Museum of Decorative Arts and Design, Oslo
OK 248-1991

32

Paul Poiret began designing luxurious capes and evening wraps, as opulent as the gowns worn underneath, in about 1907, and other designers such as Madame Paquin soon followed suit. The fashion for such glamorous formal outwear continued through the 1920s and Queen Maud had a wardrobe of evening capes.

This example is made of cerise silk overlaid with black tulle embroidered with black beads and sequins in a striking zigzag pattern. Around the neck is a beautiful collar of cerise silk roses. Such a feature may have been the choice of Queen Maud, who like many an English princess, loved her garden.

Detail of an evening gown, *c*.1921

POSSIBLY BY BAROLET, LONDON

The National Museum of Art/
Museum of Decorative Arts and Design, Oslo
OK 249-1991

This detail of a dress made in about 1921 illustrates the elaborate embroidery and beading characteristic of Queen Maud's evening gowns. The golden tawny colour of the dress was probably a deliberate choice as brown was apparently one her favourite colours.[8] Enhancing the colour are round orange beads and golden yellow glass rods. The dress is embroidered with flowers in shades of deep pink, purple, violet, blue and jade green. A blue velvet flower with brown and russet leaves completes the adornment.

Thanks to the notebook in which Queen Maud's dressers recorded information about the clothes and jewels she wore on special occasions, much more is known about her evening dresses after 1920 than before this period. Nevertheless, only a few of her surviving dresses of the 1920s can be linked to specific occasions. A 'brown sequinned dress', was worn by Maud for several occasions in 1921, including a ball in Kristiania (Oslo), a dinner party and a Christmas ball, both at Sandringham, and may be this one. Despite the beads, sequins and silk embroidery, the dress shown here is probably too simple to have been a ball gown, although it may well have served as a dinner dress. The attribution to Barolet is based on the dressers' notes, which credit 'the brown sequinned dress' to that company.

Evening dress, 1920–23

The National Museum of Art/
Museum of Decorative Arts and Design, Oslo
OK 183-1991

This sleeveless and low-cut dress of machine-made lace has an Egyptian-inspired pattern of birds, hieroglyphics and horizontal bands in silver on a pinky beige background. With its columnar cut, pointed train and horizontal draperies held with a velvet flower on the hip, the dress recalls the evening fashions of 1922–3 and illustrates that Queen Maud readily embraced these new styles. Looking at the slender cuts and youthful styles of the dresses from the early 1920s in her wardrobe, it is difficult to remember that she had turned fifty in 1919.

The fabric fits a date of 1922–3, as the Egyptian pattern was especially popular after the discovery of Tutankhamun's tomb in 1922. The skirt, however, is shorter than normal for eveningwear at the time. Dress lengths varied considerably throughout the 1920s, rising to the knee by 1925 and dropping again in 1928. Hemlines witnessed large local variations and were often shorter in Paris than in London. To complicate the issue, several of Queen Maud's gowns show evidence of having been shortened, making it difficult to date the garments in her wardrobe solely on the length of the skirt.

Evening dress and train, early 1920s

The National Museum of Art/
Museum of Decorative Arts and Design, Oslo
OK 168-1991 and OK 414-1991

This elegant gown, which is embroidered and beaded in shades of mother-of-pearl, illustrates the compromise Queen Maud adopted in accommodating formal requirements for a train and the short hemlines of 1920s eveningwear. On her earlier formal dresses, the skirt extended into a train at the back. However, such a treatment for the short styles of the 1920s would have looked rather strange. The train here is a separate garment worn attached at the shoulders, enhancing the waistless cut and vertical lines of the dress.

The design of the fabric, which incorporates huge, multi-petalled chrysanthemums, is inspired by the embroidery on early twentieth-century Chinese export shawls, while the 'dragon-scale' treatment of the petals recalls Japanese textiles of this period. Many 1920s evening dresses were designed specifically for dancing, most particularly for the new dance, the Charleston, which became the rage in 1923. They were decorated with rows of fringes, which shimmered as the wearer danced. Queen Maud's dress is far too formal for such activity, but it does sport a fashionable golden fringe, which finishes the irregular edge of the fabric at the hem.

Three evening gowns, 1929

BLANCQUAERT, LONDON (LEFT),
REVILLE-TERRY, LONDON (CENTRE)

The National Museum of Art/
Museum of Decorative Arts and Design, Oslo
OK 167-1991, OK 216-1991, OK 221-1991

These three gowns were worn by Queen Maud during the celebrations for the wedding of her son Crown Prince Olav and his Swedish cousin Princess Märtha in March 1929. All the dresses are sleeveless and low cut, with relatively loose bodices, low or no waistlines, and asymmetrical hemlines falling into points. They exemplify the most fashionable styles for evening dress in the year when Queen Maud reached sixty years of age.

The dress in the centre, made by Reville-Terry, was worn for a ball at the palace held on 19 March, which formally began the wedding celebration. The fabric of the dress is transparent chiffon bearing pale grey velvet leaves, printed with a floral motif in shades of blue and pink, orange, dark brown and black. Transparent glass beads and diamanté applied in a scalloped pattern enhance the dress. A velvet bow with long blue and purple ends attached to the left hip adds a vibrant accent.

Queen Maud wore the dress on the left by Blancquaert to a gala performance at the National Theatre on 20 March. Made from beige and gold lace, it is embroidered with a radiating design of golden glass beads edged with metal beads. A pink petticoat worn underneath enhances the lace and highlights the gold embroidery of the dress.

The blue dress on the right was probably worn for a ball at the British Legation on 17 March. The skirt ends in flounces of coarse tulle, contrasting with the shimmering effect of the beaded fabric above.

Evening gown, 1930

The National Museum of Art/
Museum of Decorative Arts and Design, Oslo
OK 17-1962

Queen Maud wore this dress for the Norwegian Royal Family's Silver Jubilee in 1930. It was made of gold brocade with pink and violet flowers, shaded in grey, beige and gold. The skirt has bias-cut insertions, characteristic of women's fashion during this decade. With its tightly fitting, sleeveless bodice and long skirt flaring out at the hemline, the dress is a fine example of the new evening fashions that began the 1930s. As such a style enhanced Queen Maud's figure and made her look taller, it was one she readily adopted.

Evening dress, *c.*1932

The National Museum of Art/
Museum of Decorative Arts and Design, Oslo
OK 33-1962

While Queen Maud avoided the extremes of late-1930s haute couture, such as the wide shoulders and Surrealist touches of Elsa Schiaparelli, other contemporary influences are evident in her wardrobe. The early 1930s saw a return to classicism in fashion, and designers such as Augustabernard, Vionnet and Lanvin created draped, columnar interpretations of antique dress. The simple, elegant lines of 1930s classicism suited Queen Maud's taste in dress. With its asymmetrical neckline and gathered bodice, and drapery and folds at the left-hand side of the waist, this dark green velvet evening gown characterizes the new chic. The reference to antiquity is all in the cut of the garment and forms an interesting contrast to the classicism of Queen Maud's evening gown 'Arlesienne' by Worth of 1912–13 (page 82).

Evening dress, 1930—35

The National Museum of Art/
Museum of Decorative Arts and Design, Oslo
OK 18-1962

40

While Queen Maud clearly liked the draped, figure-defining lines of early 1930s classicism, she also had a taste for the brightly patterned textiles of the decade. This evening gown is made of printed chiffon. The multi-coloured floral design is enhanced with beading and stands out against the very dark blue background.

Bright floral prints on a black ground were extremely popular in the 1930s. Such patterns had been pioneered during the 1920s by Atelier Martine, the school of textile design established in 1911 by Paul Poiret. By the 1930s its influence had been absorbed into mainstream textile design.

Evening dress, *c.*1935

POSSIBLY BY REVILLE-TERRY, LONDON

The National Museum of Art/
Museum of Decorative Arts and Design, Oslo
OK 72-1991

This striking evening gown of the mid-1930s is very simple
in style and cut, relying entirely on the clever arrangement
of the striped fabric for its visual impact. The sheer chiffon
in stripes of pale grey and blue is layered over itself in the
body of the gown, and the upper layer draped on the bias
so that the stripes run in a spiral. At the hem, inserts of
fabric at right angles to the stripes create fullness for the
skirt, as well as a contrast in direction to the lines of blue
and grey. The well-known textile designer Sonia Delauney
used strongly coloured stripes on sheer fabrics in the 1920s,
and the influence of this design continued into the next
decade. This example is more subdued in colouring, but
exploits the characteristics of such directional patterning.
Reville-Terry are thought to be the makers of the gown
based on information from the dressers' notes. These
indicate that Queen Maud wore an evening dress of blue
and silver-grey striped chiffon from Reville-Terry on
Midsummer's Eve 1935.

41

Evening dress, 1937

BLANCQUAERT, LONDON

The National Museum of Art/
Museum of Decorative Arts and Design, Oslo
OK 31-1962

42   An unusual colour combination and skilled use of appliqué are the eye-catching features of this evening gown of the late 1930s by the London fashion house Blancquaert. Made of brown, leaf-patterned lace, the skirt of the gown has several inserted gores. The bodice with elbow-length, puffed sleeves has a V-neckline emphasized by a green silk bow. Brown silk leaves are appliquéd on the sleeves and the skirt. Green silk lines the décolleté and shimmers under the brown lace at knee height.

  According to her dressers' notes, Queen Maud wore this gown to the theatre several times, the short sleeves of the gown providing the appropriate degree of coverage for this type of evening event.

Evening dress and jacket, *c.*1935

The National Museum of Art/
Museum of Decorative Arts and Design, Oslo
OK 27-1962 and OK 35-1962

Queen Maud attended the coronation of her nephew George VI in 1937, in her role as a British princess and as the last living offspring of Edward VII. The ceremonies required a number of garments, and all the dresses worn by Queen Maud at the various balls, banquets and dinners have been preserved. Despite differences in cut, detailing and fabrics, they are all similar in style, having fitted, normally sleeveless bodices with square necklines at the front and long, fairly tight skirts ending in trains. Just as the evening dresses worn in her first years in Norway were called 'princess style'; these dresses from the end of her life can be designated 'Queen Maud style'.

Queen Maud wore this gown for a ball at Buckingham Palace on 14 May 1937, but it may date from two years earlier, as a dress with the same description was worn for a state ball in 1935. It is made of pink silk and embroidered with small flowers and leaves in diamanté and a variety of silver glass beads. The black velvet jacket is lined with pink and has a lavish fox fur collar and cuffs.

Daywear

*'It will interest our ladies to know that
the Princess normally likes to wear simple and modest clothes.
An ordinary, plain, tailored dress is her ideal'*[1]

Queen Maud's preference for simple daywear was recorded in a booklet published on the new king and queen of Norway in 1905. Her wardrobe contains a wealth of plain dresses and smart tailored suits, even though they comprise only a fraction of the many outfits and accessories she acquired over the years.

In the context of the twenty-first century, Queen Maud's wardrobe appears to contain an excessive number of clothes. Judged by her contemporaries, however, it was not overly extensive in light of her royal role. The world that Maud grew up in was governed by the etiquette of dress, which dictated particular types of clothing for different occasions and times of day. There were morning dresses, mid-morning dresses, house dresses, walking dresses, racing dresses, visiting dresses, afternoon dresses, theatre dresses, evening dresses, gala dresses and a range of special outfits for particular sports.

In addition to formal evening events, Queen Maud had many daytime obligations, for example opening exhibitions, supporting charitable events, and attending teas and receptions for various groups of people, such as teachers and international visitors. Depending on the time of day and the formality of the occasion, any one of a widely differing range of outfits – from a tailored wool suit to a beaded silk dress – might be required.

Even more dramatic changes can be seen in Queen Maud's daywear than in her evening dresses. The most obvious is the rise of the hemline from ankle length in 1915 to just below the knee in the mid-1920s. While evening dresses retained a degree of elaboration and decoration into the 1930s, daywear became very simple and unadorned. Parisian designer Coco Chanel was particularly influential on women's fashion in the 1920s. Borrowing fabrics and styles from menswear, Chanel emphasized uncomplicated suits and coordinates of skirts, jackets and coats, with a minimum of decoration. By the end of the decade, most women relied on a wardrobe of such garments, simply cut and in plain fabrics for daytime dressing.

This development can be seen in Queen Maud's wardrobe. The change from the day dress of 1915–17 shown on page 46 to the simply cut, yet still embroidered dress of 1924–5 depicted on page 52 is startling given the span of just ten years. Within yet another decade, the embroidery has vanished and her day dresses rely on brightly printed fabrics, clever cutting and a bit of appliqué for decoration (page 55). All of these transformations occurred well after Queen Maud had turned forty years of age. Perhaps she, like many other women of the period, welcomed the simplicity of these new fashions and the liberty of movement and time they offered.

Dressing gown, *c.*1920; slippers, 1896–1909 and powder puff

National Museum of Art/
Museum of Decorative Arts and Design, Oslo
OK 740-1991, OK 694-1991, OK 855-1991

With so many different garments for specific activities and events, it was not uncommon for women to change up to five or six times a day. Royalty in particular spent a good deal of time each day dressing, restyling their hair and changing accessories and jewellery.

Queen Maud usually ate breakfast in a dressing gown such as this example of textured pink satin lined with a printed silk and trimmed with swan's down.[2] This is a very unusual survival of one of Queen Maud's most informal garments, one that none but her chambermaids and immediate family would have seen.

Summer dress, 1915–17

National Museum of Art/
Museum of Decorative Arts and Design, Oslo
OK 180-1991

This dress of between about 1915 and 1917 illustrates how elaborate women's daywear remained during the First World War. It is made of embroidered tulle and pale beige silk with a touch of pink, trimmed with fur, and was probably worn for a formal or official daytime event. During this period, fairly full skirts were fashionable, a style to which Queen Maud has made only a slight concession here. Cross-over bodices and loosely belted waists were popular stylistic elements that Maud adopted more readily. The fur trim was a fashionable detail rather than any acknowledgement of the brisk climate of Norwegian summers.

Winter dress, 1919–21

National Museum of Art/
Museum of Decorative Arts and Design, Oslo
OK 46-1962

Although Queen Maud initially resisted the wider skirts fashionable from 1915 to 1921, photographs taken in Britain illustrate that she had adapted aspects of this new style by 1919. One surviving example from this period is a blue knitted wool dress in princess style, whose simple lines belie a complex construction. Inserts at each side of the bodice continue down the skirt as panels, ending at the hem in a point edged with grey fur. The long sleeves and collar are also trimmed with fur. While contemporary fashion illustrations show quite loose waistlines or none at all, this example demonstrates more emphasis on Maud's famously small waist. She may have worn the dress at the royal winter residence, Kongsseteren, in the hills above Kristiania (Oslo), where she normally stayed in February and March.

Coat, 1919–21

National Museum of Art/
Museum of Decorative Arts and Design, Oslo
OK 127-1991

48

The dramatic juxtaposition of red and black is a striking feature of this wool coat from between 1919 and 1921. The stark contrast of the colours is mirrored in the buttons. Those closing the coat are red with narrow black borders, while the smaller buttons on the pocket flaps have black centres and wider red edges.

The loose, wide shape of the coat and bat-wing sleeves are typical of the simple, unconstructed shapes of women's dress just after the end of the First World War. The fashions of the 1920s contrasted greatly with those of Queen Maud's youth. The voluptuous silhouette of the Edwardian age was gone; now the feminine ideal was a boyish figure. Maud's petite frame easily accommodated the new straight-up-and-down lines of dress, although the latest styles of the decade no longer accentuated a small waist.

Jacket, 1920–25

National Museum of Art/
Museum of Decorative Arts and Design, Oslo
OK 40-1962

Strong colours, dramatic contrasts and abstract patterning characterized dress fabrics of the 1920s. Such features appeared a decade earlier under the influence of the costumes of the Ballets Russes, and continued for at least another fifteen years. French fashion designers such as Chanel and Patou were influenced by motifs from Russian folklore, while Lanvin looked to Aztec art for inspiration. Also influential were the abstract designs of Cubist art.

Several garments in Queen Maud's wardrobe illustrate these new textile designs. The machine embroidery on this black jacket from the early 1920s is worked in a geometric design. The red, beige and orange stripes rise in sharp peaks across the jacket. This staccato rhythm is strengthened by the lower edge of the stripes, which are jagged liked rows of icicles. A row of long fringing softens the abrupt finish of the pattern at the hem.

Afternoon dress, 1923–4

National Museum of Art/
Museum of Decorative Arts and Design, Oslo
OK 112-1991

The embroidery design on this day dress combines strap-work and pointed arches with curvilinear floral patterns. Such distinctive ornament may have been inspired by Islamic and Renaissance textile designs of the type that Fortuny copied in the 1920s. The colour combination of violet and red illustrates Queen Maud's taste for striking contrasts. The style of the dress is starkly geometric, with a horizontally layered skirt, dropped waist bodice and long, loose sleeves, and it is very typical of the early 1920s. Once almost of ankle length, the hem was taken up later in the 1920s as skirt lengths rose.

This dress is thought to correspond with one described in the dressers' notebook. A dress of 'violet and tomato-red' was worn by Queen Maud on Midsummer Night's Eve in 1924 and on her birthday in the same year.

Day dress, 1924–5

National Museum of Art/
Museum of Decorative Arts and Design, Oslo
OK 198-1991

Detail
(opposite)

The very simple style of 1920s fashion is seen in this beaded day dress of the middle of the decade. All shaping of the garment has vanished, and the shift-style dress falls straight from the shoulders and has short, straight sleeves and a wide, round neckline. Such an uncomplicated shape provided a perfect ground for the geometric beading in bronze, copper-coloured glass and gold metal beads. The intricate design is based on small squares linked into complex and interlocking shapes, inspired perhaps by folk embroidery and the abstract patterning of Art Deco.

Although the style of the dress is very plain, the silk fabric and elaborate adornment indicate that it was probably worn for public events during the day.

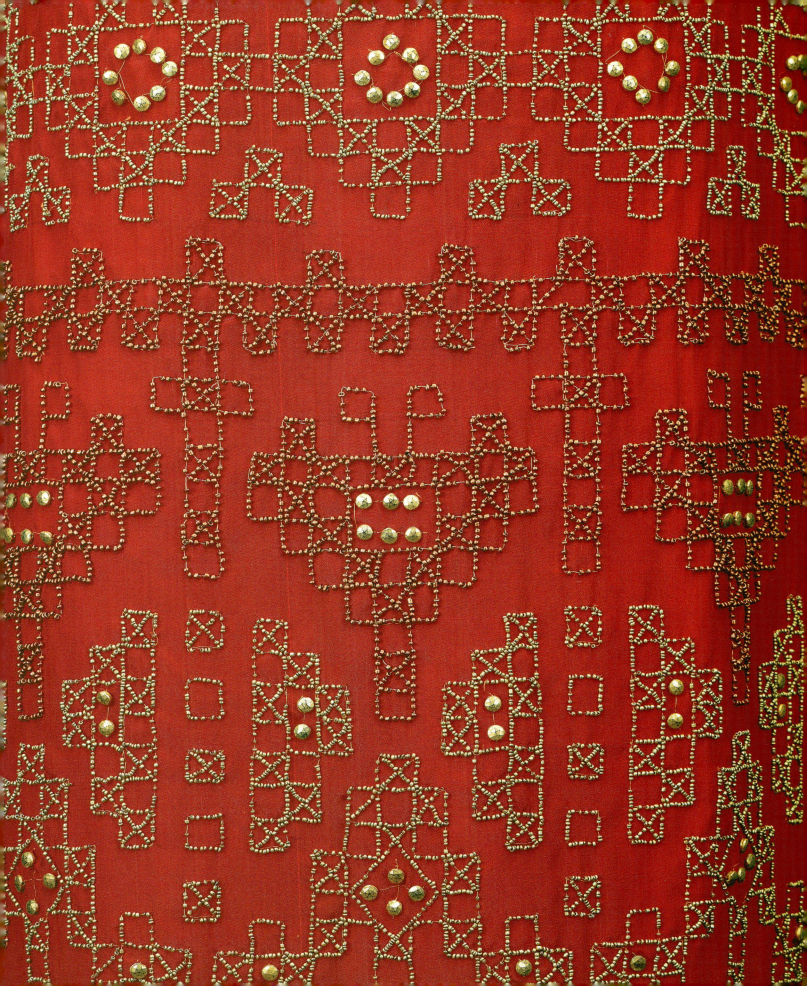

Day dress and coat, 1930

National Museum of Art/
Museum of Decorative Arts and Design, Oslo
OK 108-1991

A popular style for daytime during the 1930s was a dress
and coat of matching or coordinating materials, combining
the simple structure of the suit with the elegance of lighter
dress fabrics. Slightly more formal than a wool suit or a day
dress, such outfits found a place in Queen Maud's
wardrobe. In this example, a red, brown and beige silk
printed in a horizontal abstract design relies on the direction
of the pattern for visual interest. Bands of fabric with the
pattern moving in an opposite direction edge the front of
the coat, the wrists and the dropped waist. On the dress,
bands of patterned silk cross the bodice and the hips, diagonally encircling the torso. The subtle yet striking manipula-
tion of the fabric displays the highly skilled dressmaking that
characterizes Queen Maud's clothes.

Day dress, 1932–4

National Museum of Art/
Museum of Decorative Arts and Design, Oslo
OK 75-1991

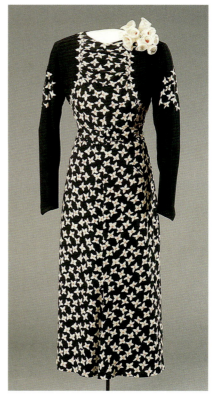

Exceptional dressmaking skills have been used in the making of this elegant silk day dress. It is made of a plain black silk and a black silk patterned with white, star-shaped flowers each with a red centre. The sleeves of plain black are set deep into the bodice. Where the two materials meet, a row of flowers, cut from the patterned silk, has been appliquéd over the curving seams. More appliqué flowers adorn the centres of the upper sleeves. While the patterns of dress fabrics and corresponding construction of women's clothing changed radically in the first three decades of the twentieth century, the highly developed sewing skills of haute couture were clearly still in use.

A long, tapered jacket made of the same patterned silk, with elbow-length cape sleeves, accompanies this dress.

Formal afternoon dress and jacket, 1935

National Museum of Art/
Museum of Decorative Arts and Design, Oslo
OK 172-1991, OK 157-1991

56 'Do you think you *c*[oul]*d* tell me what I am to come to for the Jubilee, as I want to get my clothes, I did write to George about it, but haven't yet got an answer. I *hope* I won't be in the way, & please don't trouble about *me* for *all* the ceremonies & only what you & George wish me to do, & if I am to go to the St Paul's thanksgiving Service? & what *to wear*?'[3]

Queen Maud never left her choice in clothing to chance, as indicated in this excerpt from a letter she wrote to Queen Mary a month before the celebrations of the Silver Jubilee of her brother George V. Her long correspondence with Mary records Maud's ongoing concern that she be appropriately dressed for all occasions, especially royal and official ones.

For the Thanksgiving Service in St Paul's Cathedral on 6 May 1935 she wore this ensemble of a floor-length, long-sleeved dress in pink silk lace, and a pink satin jacket with a pink fur collar. The collar is made from a whole fox fur with head, paws and tail, which is decorated with a bouquet of artificial flowers. A beige hat with pink feathers sets off the whole outfit. Compared with the other outfits in Queen Maud's wardrobe, this example seems uncharacteristically old-fashioned, indeed a cliché of the 1930s obsession with having whole animals draped around the neck, now so disconcerting to twenty-first century tastes. Perhaps it was the very formal nature of the church ceremony that required such a conventional ensemble. Nevertheless, it appears to be an exception to Maud's otherwise firmly held conviction that older women did not have to dress conservatively.

Three suits, 1930s

POSSIBLY WORTH, LONDON; REVILLE-TERRY, LONDON; AND BLANCQUAERT, LONDON

National Museum of Art/
Museum of Decorative Arts and Design, Oslo
OK 117-1991, OK 119-1991, OK 118-1991

58   Warm, practical and hard-wearing tweed suits for women had been a speciality of British ladies' tailors since Queen Maud's childhood and an example from her trousseau survives (page 94). Her wardrobe of the 1930s included checked, striped and single-colour suits in many styles. Queen Maud wore this type of garment in the garden or for walking. In addition, such outfits were appropriate for travelling, when she went to Britain by boat from Bergen, and for attending sporting events such as those held at the racetracks.

The suit on the left matches a description in the dressers' notes of a Worth outfit worn in 1938. It combines a plain blue tweed skirt with a jacket made of a plaid with a corresponding blue ground and pale blue and red checks.

On the right is a suit consisting of a cape, jacket and skirt enlivened by contrasting colours, made by the British fashion house Blancquaert. It is made of a blue-green tweed with a contrasting red lining and edging on the cape, and buttons covered in red material on the jacket and skirt, as well as a red blouse.

The suit in the centre was made by the London fashion house W.W. Reville-Terry in the early 1930s. Here, brown wool in beige stripes and checks is used in an interesting way. The stripes run vertically on the skirt and horizontally on the waistcoat, while the short coat bears a combination of the two designs in the form of a beige check. Such an inventive use of stripes looks forward to the English tailor Tommy Nutter's horizontal pin-stripe suit of 1983.[4]

Reville & Rossiter was formed in 1905 by William Wallace Terry (who took on the professional name of Reville) and Sarah Rossiter, former employees of Jay's department store.[5] In 1910 the company was appointed court dressmakers to Queen Mary and made her coronation gown the following year.[6] William Terry bought out Sarah Rossiter in 1912, but continued the company with the name Reville & Rossiter.[7] In 1919, the name changed to Reville Ltd.[8]

From the advertisements in *Vogue*, it appears that Reville was featuring designs by the French designer Elspeth Champcommunal as early as 1924 on a seasonal basis.[9] By 1928, the company had split, forming Reville Ltd run by Edward Symonds and W.W. Reville-Terry Ltd operated by William Wallace Reville Terry.[10] Queen Maud began buying evening gowns (page 41), afternoon dresses and suits from the latter company in 1929. Elspeth Champcommunal continued to design for Reville-Terry in the early thirties.[11] In 1936, Reville-Terry took over the operation of Worth in London; the two companies were listed at 50 Grosvenor Square. William Wallace Reville Terry died in 1948 at the age of seventy-eight and his company closed the following year.[12]

Formal day dress, 1930–35

National Museum of Art/
Museum of Decorative Arts and Design, Oslo
OK 225-1991

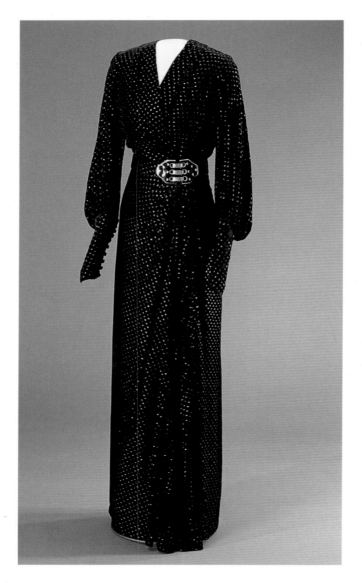

This stunning black velvet gown with a black metallic pattern was worn for formal events during the day. In contrast to the glittering evening dresses of the 1930s, there are other floor-length gowns in Queen Maud's wardrobe with long sleeves and higher necklines. These were often worn at occasions such as formal morning engagements, ceremonies held in church like the christening of her grandchildren or weddings, and garden parties. Many of them follow the style that Maud favoured: figure defining, with long-sleeved bodices and narrow skirts, sometimes flaring out at the hemlines.

Black was not usually appropriate for garden parties or weddings, so this dress may have been worn by Queen Maud at times when she was in mourning.

Three suits, 1930s

POSSIBLY WORTH, LONDON; REVILLE-TERRY, LONDON; AND BLANCQUAERT, LONDON

National Museum of Art/
Museum of Decorative Arts and Design, Oslo
OK 117-1991, OK 119-1991, OK 118-1991

58 Warm, practical and hard-wearing tweed suits for women had been a speciality of British ladies' tailors since Queen Maud's childhood and an example from her trousseau survives (page 94). Her wardrobe of the 1930s included checked, striped and single-colour suits in many styles. Queen Maud wore this type of garment in the garden or for walking. In addition, such outfits were appropriate for travelling, when she went to Britain by boat from Bergen, and for attending sporting events such as those held at the racetracks.

The suit on the left matches a description in the dressers' notes of a Worth outfit worn in 1938. It combines a plain blue tweed skirt with a jacket made of a plaid with a corresponding blue ground and pale blue and red checks.

On the right is a suit consisting of a cape, jacket and skirt enlivened by contrasting colours, made by the British fashion house Blancquaert. It is made of a blue-green tweed with a contrasting red lining and edging on the cape, and buttons covered in red material on the jacket and skirt, as well as a red blouse.

The suit in the centre was made by the London fashion house W.W. Reville-Terry in the early 1930s. Here, brown wool in beige stripes and checks is used in an interesting way. The stripes run vertically on the skirt and horizontally on the waistcoat, while the short coat bears a combination of the two designs in the form of a beige check. Such an inventive use of stripes looks forward to the English tailor Tommy Nutter's horizontal pin-stripe suit of 1983.[4]

Reville & Rossiter was formed in 1905 by William Wallace Terry (who took on the professional name of Reville) and Sarah Rossiter, former employees of Jay's department store.[5] In 1910 the company was appointed court dressmakers to Queen Mary and made her coronation gown the following year.[6] William Terry bought out Sarah Rossiter in 1912, but continued the company with the name Reville & Rossiter.[7] In 1919, the name changed to Reville Ltd.[8]

From the advertisements in *Vogue*, it appears that Reville was featuring designs by the French designer Elspeth Champcommunal as early as 1924 on a seasonal basis.[9] By 1928, the company had split, forming Reville Ltd run by Edward Symonds and W.W. Reville-Terry Ltd operated by William Wallace Reville Terry.[10] Queen Maud began buying evening gowns (page 41), afternoon dresses and suits from the latter company in 1929. Elspeth Champcommunal continued to design for Reville-Terry in the early thirties.[11] In 1936, Reville-Terry took over the operation of Worth in London; the two companies were listed at 50 Grosvenor Square. William Wallace Reville Terry died in 1948 at the age of seventy-eight and his company closed the following year.[12]

Detail of a suit, *c.*1937

62

In addition to the thick tweed suits, lighter woollen and silk suits from the late 1930s survive in Queen Maud's wardrobe. Several of them are quite similar in basic shape, with short, tapered jackets and straight or gored skirts. However, each is made individual by variety in fabrics, detail and trim. The front opening, hem and cuffs of this blue woollen suit are scalloped and edged in pink, adding an elegant finish to an otherwise plain suit. Instead of having buttons, the jacket is closed with ties bound in an intricate frog on either side of the front.

The binding of the scalloped edges in such a narrow edge would have required extremely careful hand sewing. Similar skill was involved in the fine finishing and knotting of the ties. These details are another example of the very high-quality sewing and couture techniques that went into all of Queen Maud's clothes.

Tea gown, early 1930s

National Museum of Art/
Museum of Decorative Arts and Design, Oslo
OK 30-1962

After breakfast and her morning ride, Queen Maud changed to a simple mid-morning suit or dress. She kept these clothes on throughout the day if she did not have guests for lunch or afternoon tea. For a private errand or an official engagement, more formal day clothes would be worn. At the end of the afternoon Maud often changed into a tea gown, and wore it for an hour or so before changing for dinner. She always wore an evening dress for dinner if King Haakon was present. If, however, she was alone, she often dined in a tea gown, such as this example in black velvet trimmed with fur from the early 1930s. It is loosely constructed, fastening with a braided loop at the left side, and has long sleeves with an extended cuff, in imitation of the 'hanging sleeves' of medieval dress.

Sportswear

'… & we lived out of doors & went on skis
& tobogganed & sleighed,…'[1]

Throughout her life, Queen Maud took part in and clearly loved a variety of sports. She was an eager rider and just as enthusiastic about skiing. She also cycled, played tennis, went ice- and roller-skating and enjoyed tobogganing. Through these activities we can glimpse the private side of her life and personal pleasures.

Queen Maud was fortunate that she was born at a time when sports for women were becoming widely accepted. Beginning with croquet in the 1860s, tennis, archery and yachting in the 1870s and cycling in the 1890s, sports gradually became accepted activities, in the same way that piano playing and watercolour painting were considered suitable hobbies for young women.

Such activity had its radical associations, however, for both the dress-reform movement and fledgling feminist groups advocated sports for women in order to improve physical health, as a foundation for a wider public role in life. One of the contentious issues in society was the clothing worn by women in general and specifically for sports. How far could it reject fashionable styles for the sake of safety and freedom of movement? Sporting dress was one of the first areas where women could forsake a corset, shorten their skirts or don trousers when to do so otherwise was still socially unacceptable.

At the time of Princess Maud's wedding in 1896, British magazines praised her great interest in sport and reported that she rode, cycled and skated. Nevertheless, the fashion magazine *The Queen* reassured its readers that Maud had never worn a 'rational costume', or anything resembling it (in other words, bloomers), when she cycled.[2] The cycling ensemble made for her trousseau by Messrs Godfray and Dart of London comprised a jacket and skirt. The latter had little pockets at the hemline that could be weighted with shot to keep the skirt from blowing up on windy days.[3] While Queen Maud pursued a variety of sports right to the end of her life, she pioneered no radical sportswear and, for the most part, kept to the styles of sporting dress that had been customary in her youth.

King Haakon
and Queen Maud
skiing, 1906
Wilse/Norsk
Folkemuseum, Oslo

Riding habit, 1920,
altered 1924 and 1926, with boots and hat

BUSVINE, LONDON

The National Museum of Art/
Museum of Decorative Arts and Design, Oslo
OK 68-1962, OK 110-1962 and OK 108-1962

For centuries, riding was the one form of exercise deemed socially acceptable for women. The sport had a strong tradition in Britain, and it was natural that Queen Maud learned to ride as a child. It was an activity that she enjoyed immensely and continued throughout her life. Weather and location permitting, she went riding every day in Norway as well as at Appleton House.

Traditionally, a woman's riding habit was made by a tailor rather than a dressmaker, and borrowed the tailored coat and waistcoat that men wore, matching them with a petticoat. Like a man's suit, a woman's riding habit was made of fine wool, usually in dark colours. During the nineteenth century, the skirt of the habit was specially cut and tailored to fit over the legs while seated side-saddle, in a style known as an apron skirt. The riding habits left by Queen Maud all date from the 1920s and 1930s, with skirts of the apron type. They are expertly cut, with tailor-made quality down to the last detail. The jackets are closely fitted and single breasted, with long, tight sleeves.

In the 1890s, some daring women started to ride astride rather than side-saddle. Initially they wore long, divided skirts, similar to those worn by female cyclists, and then adopted jodhpurs as worn by men, but with long riding coats on top to hide them entirely. Nonetheless, it was not generally accepted in Britain for women to ride astride wearing trousers until after the First World War. Throughout her life, Queen Maud was true to the mode of riding and clothing that she had been used to as a child. In Norway, most female riders started riding astride in the 1920s; towards the end of the 1930s, Queen Maud was said to be the only female rider still riding side-saddle.

According to the London directories, Busvine began as tailors in 1881 and remained in business until 1951. By 1883, the company had a royal warrant to provide riding habits for the Princess of Wales, and later supplied the same for a number of European courts. Busvine made the riding habits for Princess Maud's trousseau when she married in 1896, and all the habits preserved in her wardrobe. The company remained an expert in this field well into the twentieth century, and a shopping guide of 1934 recommended it as the place to go to for riding habits.[4] Unlike other fashion houses founded in the late nineteenth century, which declined after the First World War, Busvine expanded during this period. By the 1930s, it had branches in Berlin, Paris and New York, and its advertisements in *Vogue* emphasized tailored daywear and furs.[5]

Dress for winter sports, early 1920s

VERNON, LONDON

The National Museum of Art/
Museum of Decorative Arts and Design, Oslo
OK 43-1962

Norway is regarded as the birthplace of modern skiing, and skis can be traced far back in Norwegian history as a means of transport for women and men. Whether King Haakon and Queen Maud considered skiing as the epitome of Norwegianness is not known, but they were tobogganing and skiing very soon after their arrival in 1905. While their eagerness to learn may have been a desire to demonstrate that they wanted to become Norwegian, it must have been their love of cross-country skiing that kept them dedicated to it for so many years. From 1910 on, Maud went skiing twice a day, when weather permitted, during her winter sojourns at the royal residence Kongsseteren at Voksen-kollen, in the hills above Kristiania (Oslo).

While a few more daring women skied in trousers before 1910, most wore shortened full skirts with jackets for the sport. Photographs from Queen Maud's first years in Norway show that she dressed in this manner for skiing, wearing a full ankle-length skirt and a light, high-necked jumper (see page 64). She probably wore either long trousers or knee breeches under her skirt, a combination borrowed from the riding habit.

Maud also wore dresses and coats for skiing, and several examples from the 1920s were made for the sport. This black-checked, blue dress from the London ladies' tailor Vernon, was worn for skiing and tobogganing. The long, tight sleeves and closely fitting bodice kept out the cold, while the slightly full skirt allowed free movement of the legs.

Coat for winter sports, 1920–25

BLANCQUAERT, LONDON

The National Museum of Art/
Museum of Decorative Arts and Design, Oslo
OK 39-1962

Queen Maud
tobogganing,
1910–12
Det Kongelige
Slott, Oslo

This thick wool, fur-trimmed coat was worn by Queen Maud for skiing and tobogganing in the 1920s. The high, tightly closing collar was designed to protect against a cold wind. At a time when coats were generally waistless and loose in style (compare with the coat on page 48), this style is an adaptation specifically for skiing. Although very practical in cut and materials, the coat is beautifully trimmed. Strips of the brown woollen fabric have been stitched with narrow gaps between them over red wool, so that fine lines of red flash at the pocket and cuff. Such attention to detail is typical of couture production, and this coat was made by the London fashion house Blancquaert. Under the coat, Maud probably wore a skirt with knee-length breeches as well as a jumper. She sometimes wore a long windcheater over her ski coat.

Queen Maud's love of tobogganing continued throughout her life. Not content with shallow slopes, she took on ever more challenging terrain such as the steep, curved tobogganing slope known as 'The Corkscrew', which descends the hills not far from Kongsseteren. The photograph above, taken between 1910 and 1912, shows Maud tobogganing at high speed down one of the hills at Kongsseteren. One of the family dogs is running alongside, and her spontaneous smile conveys her childlike delight.

Skiing outfit, *c.*1935

FRODE BRAATHEN, OSLO

The National Museum of Art/
Museum of Decorative Arts and Design, Oslo
OK 71-1962

By the 1930s, even Queen Maud wore trousers on the piste. This smart, tailor-made gabardine suit is typical of the ski fashions of the early 1930s. The dark brown suit has a jacket with a belt at the waist, pockets with big, decorative flaps and a removable, fur-lined hood. The long trousers are quite wide, making them comfortable to wear, and they are held together at the ankles to stop the snow from getting in. Towards the end of the 1920s, ski suits with long trousers were launched for women in Norway, and this style would dominate the 1930s.

When Queen Maud changed from a skiing coat to a ski suit, it was the first time that she dared show herself publicly in 'men's clothing', an act remarkable for a woman born in 1869. By this time, many women had been skiing in trousers for at least twenty years, and some for even longer. Maud's royal position, however, made her retain traditional attire for many years. When she did change to ski trousers in the 1930s, it may have been because almost all female skiers in Norway were wearing trousers and she did not want to stand out by dressing differently.

The Frode Braathen firm was in operation between 1933 and 1945, with its first premises on the main street in Oslo. Sports clothing was one of the specialities of the company, and many of its ski suits were depicted in the periodical *Vi Selv og våre hjem* (Ourselves and our home) in the 1930s. In 1936, Frode Braathen advertised primarily skiing wear. Clients could order the company's own designs for sporting garments, Parisian models and furs. Several of his sports models were sold to fashion houses abroad – in 1934, for example, Patou in Paris bought four Frode Braathen skiing outfits.[6]

Accessories

*'Messrs. Atloff and Norman, in New Bond Street,
have provided all her boots and shoes, and the variety
is both great and pretty.'*[1]

Princess Maud's trousseau included a huge range of accessories: gold, silver and bronze shoes; nut brown, tan and black walking shoes; riding and travelling boots; suede and satin shoes; 'gloves for all weathers and occasions'; and a plethora of bonnets and hats. With five or six changes of dress each day throughout her life, Maud needed a wide selection of accessories to complete her ensembles. Each of the daywear outfits illustrated in this book would have required shoes and stockings, hat, handbag, gloves and, in some instances, scarves and blouses.

In order to keep track of the accessories that went with each ensemble, Queen Maud relied on her dressers. One of their tasks was taking care of the queen's wardrobe and jewellery, keeping them tidy and ensuring that everything was in good order. If necessary, they made simple repairs or alterations to garments. In addition, they often helped Maud change, undoing and doing up the many press-studs and hooks and eyes that fastened her clothes, particularly evening gowns. When travelling, Maud often had as many as fifty suitcases with her, the packing done by the dressers, who ensured that the correct accessories were included for each ensemble. The rare occasions when Queen Maud was separated from her baggage could leave her distinctly embarrassed, as in 1926 when she stopped in Denmark on her way home from Britain. Her brother-in-law King Christian and his wife Queen Alexandrine held a big dinner for her, but alas, 'I hadn't *even* a change of dress as *all* my luggage got left behind at Herhestahl, & we only found it out at Hamburg, so you can imagine *my* despair!'[2]

Looking at all of Queen Maud's gloves and shoes, many of which appear to be only barely used, and all the clothes for different occasions, one wonders how many times she wore each outfit. The dressers' notebooks show that some gowns for the grandest occasions were worn only once, but most were wore two or three times, or even more. When Queen Maud's clothes were no longer suitable for her use, some were given away, either to the women of court or to loyal servants. Other garments were preserved, as indicated by this collection of clothing, for sentimental reasons or because they might be worn or used again.

A number of clothes in Queen Maud's wardrobe have been altered. The alterations are usually a careful updating of style, but some outfits appear to have been almost completely remade. Parts of garments could also be reused, and at the palace there were boxes of lace, embroidery and fur that had been taken off outfits, waiting to be used again. Such prudent thrift may have been inherited from Queen Maud's mother Princess Alexandra, who had stockings and handkerchiefs darned, and was said to have had silk dresses taken apart so that they could be reused as furniture covers.[3]

Detail of blouse, 1915–17

VERNON, LONDON

The National Museum of Art/
Museum of Decorative Arts and Design, Oslo
OK 365-1991

A blouse in beige lace, lined with silk, is a more conservative example from Queen Maud's wardrobe, harking back to the elaborate styles of the Edwardian period. The blouse is edged with beige silk cording and embroidered down the centre in beige silk. Queen Maud was a customer of Vernon for many years, ordering a wide range of clothes from the company.

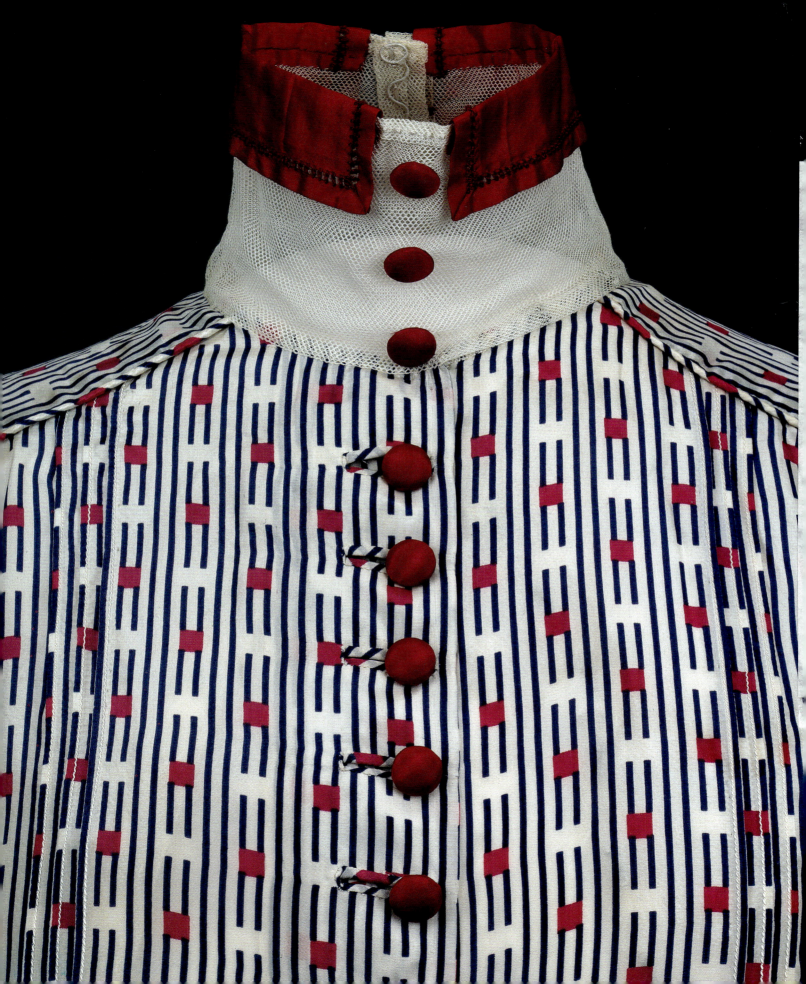

Detail of blouse, 1914–16

MADAME CLAPHAM, HULL

The National Museum of Art/
Museum of Decorative Arts and Design, Oslo
OK 299-1991

This eye-catching blouse with a bold pattern of stripes and blocks of colour illustrates the presence of abstract, geometric designs in dress fabrics early in the twentieth century. While Queen Maud normally patronized London and Paris designers and fashion houses, this example was made by a dressmaker, Madame Clapham, who ran her business in Hull. When Queen Maud began buying from Madame Clapham is unknown, but outfits made by her are mentioned in the dressers' notes from 1921 and continue until at least 1933. Maud's custom may have begun much earlier, as Madame Clapham stated that she made clothing for royalty in an interview in *The Hull Lady* in 1901.[4] Queen Maud was one of Madame Clapham's most loyal clients. The two of them developed a friendship beyond just business transactions, as Madame Clapham and her husband were once invited to Oslo as guests of the queen.[5]

Madame Clapham met Queen Maud regularly at either Appleton House or Claridge's Hotel in London, where the queen often stayed. They agreed on the style of various outfits and Queen Maud often gave Madame Clapham trimmings such as lace and furs to decorate particular garments. The clothing was then made in Hull and sent to her by post or rail when finished. Madame Clapham made a variety of outfits for Queen Maud, ranging from eveningwear to suits and ensembles.

Kingston-upon-Hull City Museums and Art Galleries hold a number of Madame Clapham's creations, and curators Jayne Tyler and Anne Crowther, with the help of Clare Parsons, have carried out an excellent study of the history of Madame Clapham's business, based on interviews with former staff and family members, as well as earlier research by Anne Crowther.[6] The publication *Madame Clapham: Hull's Celebrated Dressmaker* provides exceptional detail regarding the dressmaking industry in the late nineteenth and twentieth centuries, particularly when such information is lacking for many other contemporary fashion businesses.

Emily Clapham was born in 1856. She apprenticed as a seamstress at Marshall and Snelgrove in Scarborough.[7] In 1887, with her husband's support, she opened a dressmaking shop in Hull, which was soon frequented by the city's fashionable ladies. Madame Clapham was an unusual example of a widely successful fashion house outside the dominant centres of London and Paris. Not only did she attract the custom of wealthy women in the East Riding of Yorkshire, but she also drew the patronage of a wider social circle, such as Lady Duff Cooper, the Duchess of Norfolk, Baroness Beaumont, Lady Ida Sitwell, Lady Westmoreland and, of course, Queen Maud.[8]

The heyday of Madame Clapham's business was the period between 1890 and 1914, when she employed some 150 people, with specialized departments for making dress bodices, skirts, coats and so on.[9] While not a design innovator herself, Emily Clapham can be considered an expert fashion 'interpreter'. She had a good eye for colour and design, and a flare for selecting appropriate styles for customers and occasions. Each season she would purchase Paris and London models, but these were never slavishly copied. With the help of current fashion plates, Madame Clapham created her own individual styles by borrowing elements of design from a variety of sources.[10] Her clients were offered entirely fashionable but unique garments that were considerably less expensive than a Worth or Paquin original.[11]

Interviews with seamstresses who worked for Madame Clapham illustrate the working conditions of the fashion business: the spartan workrooms, long hours, seasonal demands of production, strict hierarchy of staff, as well as the technical details and social culture of dressmaking.[12] While the precision of documentation for this particular company may be unique, it can be assumed that most fashion designers and dressmakers of the late nineteenth and early twentieth centuries operated in similar environments.

After the First World War, Madame Clapham's began to decline in the face of radical changes in fashion and competition from shops offering ready-made clothing. Remarkably, the business survived until her death in 1952. Her niece Emily Wall continued running Madame Clapham's on a smaller scale until 1967, providing a mixture of ready-made clothing purchased in London and bespoke garments.[13]

73

Shoes, hats, gloves and handbags, 1920–38

The National Museum of Art/
Museum of Decorative Arts and Design, Oslo

Most of the accessories in Queen Maud's wardrobe date from the 1930s. She favoured the fairly small hats with narrow brims popular during the decade, as they did not overwhelm her diminutive frame. These were made in a wide variety of fabrics and trims to match her many suits and day dresses.

Many pairs of gloves in a range of colours are also preserved. Until the early 1960s, gloves were an essential accessory for both men and women; one would not be seen outdoors in public without them. It was not always necessary to wear them – they could be held in the hand – but they had to be present.

The small clutch handbag was a style popular in the 1920s and 1930s, with designs inspired by Art Deco, and many examples survive in Queen Maud's wardrobe.

French Designers

*'...I must get myself 2 new dresses,
otherwise have only old ones!!'*[1]

Queen Maud's correspondence with Queen Mary reveals her awareness of the requirement to dress well, particularly on grand occasions. Her surviving wardrobe gives us great insight not only into her life and personality, but also into the businesses supplying her clothing. The unfailingly high quality of the clothes with regard to design, sewing, decoration and materials indicates that those who made them knew their trade.

Few of the garments in Queen Maud's wardrobe have retained any labels. Hilda Cooper, her dresser, said that the labels were sometimes removed because the queen did not wish to advertise for any particular fashion house, or because they were uncomfortable. The labels that remain, together with the dressers' notes, provide the names of the main fashion houses that made Maud's clothes during her years as queen.

In the nineteenth century, a woman's trousseau was her first acquisition of clothing as an adult, and sometimes the largest and most important one of her life. As a princess, Maud's trousseau was particularly significant not only to her lifestyle, but also to the public and to the fashion trade. The makers of Maud's trousseau, both French and British, were almost all suppliers to her mother Princess Alexandra and represent a wide variety of establishments, including haute couture, fashion houses, ladies' tailors, dressmakers and department stores. Maud remained faithful to most of these businesses for many years. However, as fashions changed and some companies ceased trading and others declined in importance, she sought out new dressmakers and designers, reflecting her continued interest in contemporary styles.

Queen Maud rarely frequented the business premises in person. The head of the company, or his or her representative, visited the queen with clothes or fashion sketches. The garments were made to measure, although Maud seldom attended fittings during the process. Two dressmaker's torsos made to the queen's measurements have been preserved with her wardrobe. Her most frequently patronized fashion houses probably fitted her clothes to torsos such as these. The French Bust Company Ltd, a London company, had H.M. the Queen of Norway on its list of royal and noble customers, which was used in advertising in the late 1930s.[2]

Among the makers of Queen Maud's wardrobe the company of Worth is the most famous. Charles Frederick Worth (1825–95) was *the* couturier of the nineteenth century, indeed the man credited with creating haute couture and high fashion as it is known today. He worked his way from a humble clerk in a department store in the 1840s to the arbitrator of fashionable dress in the second half of the century. His clients included the Empress Eugénie, most of the royal houses of Europe, members of America's wealthy elite and the famous actresses of the day. Queen Maud's mother Princess Alexandra was recorded by *The Queen* as having a

Worth dinner dress in 1883, and her aunt Dagmar, the Russian Tsarina, was one of Worth's most loyal customers.[3]

As the first haute couturier, Worth had unprecedented influence on contemporary fashion. Dress historians trace the crinoline, the bustle and almost every configuration of sleeve and collar of the late nineteenth century to his atelier. Thanks to the wide distribution of Worth designs through fashion plates and models, dressmakers around the world copied his styles, and even the most humble ready-made dress was a diluted version of his magnificent creations.

After his death in 1895, Worth's influence waned, partly because the genius of the business had rested in him personally and partly because younger and more inventive designers inevitably took over as leaders of fashion. The company continued under the direction of Worth's two sons, Jean-Philippe, who designed the clothes, and Gaston, who ran the business. Rather than being involved in the inventive, cutting edge of fashion design, the house of Worth now created a more understated, classically elegant style of dress and one that would have appealed to Queen Maud's tastes. Although Queen Maud bought from several Paris designers, it would appear that she always shopped from the London branch of Worth. The clothes acquired there have been included in this section, as Worth in London either sold Paris models or, even when independent in the 1930s, was run by the French designer Elspeth Champcommunal.

Queen Maud also purchased clothing from two other well-known Paris couturiers, Molyneux and Jean Patou, according to either the dressers' notes or their personal recollections. Unfortunately no labelled clothes by Molyneux remain in the collection, and none can be identified by documentation. Queen Maud purchased clothing from Patou in 1923. In her wardrobe is a jacket made of a beaded fabric with Chinese motifs from Patou's spring and summer collection that year. Patou used the same fabric in a dress named 'Nuit de Chine' but, alas, there is no mention of Patou in the dressers' notes, nor have any garments labelled Patou survived.[4] The Jean Patou house of couture, which still exists today, confirms that Queen Maud was its customer.[5] Perhaps Maud purchased some of the sportier, more youthful outfits that were Patou's speciality.

The other French fashion houses that supplied Queen Maud with clothes, Morin-Blossier and Laferrière, are less known to us now, having been eclipsed by names like Worth, Poiret and Chanel. Fashion history has concentrated on the innovators and ignored the interpreters – those who did not invent influential new styles, but made a successful career of translating fashion innovations into a variety of beautifully made clothing for a wide range of clients. An analysis of Queen Maud's wardrobe provides the opportunity to revive their reputations and establish them in the history of the fashion business.

Fancy dress costume, 1897

MORIN-BLOSSIER, PARIS

The National Museum of Art/
Museum of Decorative Arts and Design, Oslo
OK 256-1991

78

Prince Carl,
Princess Maud and
Princess Victoria at
the Devonshire
House Ball, 2 July
1897
Lafayette/Royal
Archives, Windsor

The Duchess of Devonshire's Ball was one of the social climaxes of Queen Victoria's Jubilee in 1897, hailed by the press as the greatest costume ball of the past quarter-century.[6] Some 700 royal and aristocratic guests were invited, with instructions to attend dressed in allegorical or historical costumes dating to before 1815. A hectic scramble for a suitable ensemble ensued by all. They scoured the National Gallery, the print collection of the British Museum and family portraits for images of historical dress to copy.[7] Couturiers, seamstresses and tailors in London worked around the clock throughout June 1897 in order to complete all the costumes, as did several fashion houses in Paris.

The Prince of Wales came as the Grand Prior of the Order of St John of Jerusalem and Princess Alexandra was dressed as Marguerite de Valois, wife of the future Henry IV, King of France. Princess Maud and the other women in the royal party were given roles as ladies of the court of Marguerite. All had costumes with full skirts, high standing collars and long sleeves puffed at the top, in imitation of late sixteenth-century dress.

Princess Maud's dress was made by Morin-Blossier of pink satin appliquéd with a sheer fabric of silk and silver thread in a lattice pattern. Silver sequins and silver and glass beads edge the appliqué. Diamanté forms rosettes on the gown and decorates the machine-lace collar and cuffs. Today the silver has oxidized, but the photograph hints at its original splendour even in black and white. The shimmering embroidery heightened the sparkling of the jewelled brooches on the bodice, the twinkling of Maud's miniature crown and the glittering of her pearl and diamond necklaces.

Maud's husband Prince Carl was dressed as a sixteenth-century Danish courtier with doublet, trunk hose, cloak and false beard.

Evening dress, 1906

MORIN-BLOSSIER, PARIS

The National Museum of Art/
Museum of Decorative Arts and Design, Oslo
OK 2-1962

On the day after Queen Maud's coronation, a soirée was held at Stiftsgården in Trondhjem, where the Norwegian newspaper *Morgenbladet* recorded that she was 'stunningly beautifully dressed' in this gown.[8] A spectacular example of Morin-Blossier's talents, the gown has a transparent lace overdress and sleeves of pale beige tulle embroidered with a floral motif. The lace is enriched with embroidery in metal thread, sequins, artificial pearls and diamanté. Artificial flowers outline the neck, continue down the sleeves and edge the long, loose back panel and lower edge of the skirt and train. Queen Maud also wore this dress on a state visit to France in 1907 and her choice indicates the position held by this company in the capital of fashion.[9]

Morin-Blossier was one of the largest fashion houses in Paris at the turn of the century. It was founded by Marie Blossier and Victoire Morin, seamstresses from Vienna who formed a partnership in Paris around 1879.[10] By 1881, the company was a royal supplier to Queen Maud's maternal grandmother Queen Louise.[11] In 1885, the fashion magazine *L'Art et la Mode* described Morin-Blossier as a leading Parisian fashion house known for its exquisite outfits.[12] The company supplied various outfits for Princess Maud's trousseau, including five capes and ten elegant dresses, although none survives in her wardrobe.[13] Morin-Blossier was involved in making Queen Alexandra's gowns for the coronation of 1902, although this was not reported in the British press. The silk was specially embroidered in India, under the direction of Lady Curzon. However, the presence of the Morin-Blossier label in the gown indicates that the fashion house must have at least made the final fittings.[14]

Morin-Blossier's pre-eminence in the fashion world was fairly short-lived, despite its exclusive clientele. A feature on a society wedding in *L'Art et La Mode* on 29 February 1908 seems to have been its last publicity and it probably closed shortly afterwards.

Evening dress 'Arlesienne', 1912–13

WORTH, PARIS/LONDON

The National Museum of Art/
Museum of Decorative Arts and Design, Oslo
OK 201-1991

Photograph of
'Arlesienne',
1912–13, winter
collection
AAD.1/59-1982
V&A Museum

The earliest surviving dress made by Worth for Queen Maud is this exquisite evening gown in white silk covered with tulle, beaded in white and black. Simple in style and with a high waist, the dress corresponds with the prevailing 'Directoire' designs pioneered by Paul Poiret. However, this example – with its Greek key and acanthus leaf pattern – embodies a more explicit interpretation of classicism.

In 1958, a major collection of photographs and drawings of Worth models from the Paris head office was donated to the Victoria and Albert Museum. From these, nine of Queen Maud's dresses and one suit have been identified as Worth models, including this one.

Queen Maud probably ordered this dress from the London branch of Worth. According to Jean Philippe Worth, his brother Gaston 'was responsible for the opening of our very successful branch in London in the last years of the nineteenth century. At first his idea had been to have a sort of office in that city, where our British clientele might come and order gowns to be made in Paris.'[15]

Exactly when and where in London this was established is difficult to determine. The London directories list a 'Worth & Co., corsetière, ladies outfitter and dressmaker at 4 Hanover Street, 15 Sloane Square and Brighton' from 1884 onwards. However, this seems unlikely to have been a branch of Worth Paris, if only because the term 'outfitter' implies ready-made clothing. Certainly by 1903, Worth Paris was established at 4 New Burlington Street, in premises including workrooms where clothes were made.[16] In 1911, the London branch moved again to 3 Hanover Square.[17] At the same time in Paris, Jean-Philippe Worth retired and his nephew Jean-Charles took over as designer.[18]

Day dress 'Flirt', 1938–9

WORTH, PARIS/LONDON

The National Museum of Art/
Museum of Decorative Arts and Design, Oslo
OK 98-1991

Design for 'Flirt',
1938–9, winter
collection
E.18125-1957
V&A Museum

If Queen Maud continued to shop at Worth between 'Arlesienne' of 1912–13 and 1937, when the fashion house's name appears on the dressers' notes, there are no records, and no clothes labelled with its name survive. By this time, the London branch of Worth had been taken over by W.W. Reville-Terry, located at 50 Grosvenor Street.[19] Elspeth Champcommunal became the designer for Worth London, although Paris models continued to be offered, designed by Roger Worth, who succeeded upon the retirement of his uncle Jean-Charles in 1935.[20] Queen Maud, as a customer of Reville-Terry, may have become a client of Worth again with this merger. Worth in London remained at 50 Grosvenor Street until 1959. The Paris branch was sold to Paquin in 1954 and closed completely in 1956.

This design, 'Flirt', is one of two day outfits ordered by Queen Maud from the 1938–9 winter collection. The outfits must have been ordered in London, because on the list made of the queen's clothes when they were in storage during the war, 'Splendeur' (page 88) was identified as a French model purchased in London.

By comparing the design and the dress, it is clear that Queen Maud made some modifications. The wide shoulders popularized by Elsa Schiaparelli in the mid-1930s were obviously not to Maud's taste. On the other hand, Roger Worth's designs were neither overly conservative nor radical. The very plain black silk dress is enlivened with appliqué in black velvet and red, fashioned in interlocking scrolls. Such a design is in keeping with current fashions, particularly the bold, Rococo-inspired appliqués of Schiaparelli.

That a dress as striking as this one should appeal to a woman of sixty-eight is evidence of Queen Maud's eternally fashionable tastes.

Suit 'Trotteur', 1938–9

WORTH, PARIS/LONDON

The National Museum of Art/
Museum of Decorative Arts and Design, Oslo
OK 120-1991

Design for
'Trotteur', 1938–9,
winter collection
E.18026-1957
V&A Museum

Another outfit made for Queen Maud by Worth from its winter 1938–9 collection is this suit, 'Trotteur'. Again, Maud probably modified the shoulder width from the original design. Made of plain black wool with a straight skirt and shaped jacket, the style corresponds with Queen Maud's taste. A jaunty row of black pompoms enlivens the hem and more of them trim the jacket.

Another suit that Worth probably made for Queen Maud in 1938 is shown on page 58.

Ensemble 'Splendeur', 1938

WORTH, PARIS/LONDON

The National Museum of Art/
Museum of Decorative Arts and Design, Oslo
OK 214-1991

Design for
'Splendeur', 1938,
winter collection
E.17991-1957
V&A Museum

Other identified Worth dresses in Queen Maud's wardrobe, documented in the Archive of Art and Design at the V&A, include this ensemble from the 1938 winter collection. The pink silk top with embroidered sequin borders in black, silver and gold contrasts brightly with the plain, straight black skirt. The jacket, in black silk with long sleeves, differs slightly from the drawing.

It is not entirely clear for which occasions Queen Maud wore this outfit. By the late 1930s, a floor-length skirt implied a formal evening event. However, the short jacket and casual top suggest a more informal sort of occasion, such as dinner or the theatre.

Evening gown 'Seduction', 1938

WORTH, PARIS/LONDON

The National Museum of Art/
Museum of Decorative Arts and Design, Oslo
OK 22-1962

Design for 'Seduction',
1938, winter collection
E.17993-1957
V&A Museum

The last evening dress worn by Queen Maud, in November 1938, shows her taste in clothes at its best. The dress, with a straight skirt, sleeveless bodice and V-shaped neckline, is made of black silk jersey. A comparison with the design shows that Queen Maud modified the depth of the plunging V-neckline and armholes.

The gown is decorated with three asymmetrically placed, multi-coloured floral motifs cut from another fabric. In its simplicity, long, vertical lines and sparse but refined use of decoration, the dress perfectly suited a woman who wanted to dress elegantly, fashionably and discreetly.

British Designers

In addition to the Paris couturiers, Queen Maud also patronized a number of fashion establishments in Britain. While many of her stunning ceremonial and evening dresses were made in Paris, most of her suits and tailored clothing came from London. During the nineteenth century a number of British fashion houses evolved in the shadow of Charles Worth, relying on Britain's excellent tailoring traditions to produce suits, tailored dresses and daywear for women. By the 1890s several British couture companies were producing elaborate evening gowns that rivalled the quality of Paris.

One of the most successful fashion houses in Britain was Redfern. It began as the drapery shop of John Redfern in Cowes on the Isle of Wight in the 1840s, where the business relied on the custom of Queen Victoria and her household at Osborne. During the 1870s, the Cowes Regatta became one of the most fashionable events on the social calendar. Redfern began making tailored serge dresses for women to wear on board ship. Princess Alexandra favoured Redfern yachting dresses, ensuring their popularity with a wider public. John Redfern and his sons expanded their range to include garments for other sports, such as riding, hunting, shooting and tennis, and offered a chic, tailored dress for daywear. These 'tailor-mades' became extremely fashionable and by 1890, Redfern & Sons was a leading name in haute couture, with branches throughout Britain, France and the United States. When the family incorporated as the company Redfern in 1892, it was Charles Worth's most serious competition, supplying court dress and eveningwear as well as its renowned tailor-mades to an extensive list of royal patrons and famous actresses and singers.[1]

As was the case with the Paris fashion houses, Maud's custom of London establishments began with her trousseau and suppliers patronized by her mother such as Redfern, Vernon, Busvine and Mme Duboc, to which she later added designers and dressmakers of her own choice. They represent a range of the types of fashion business in operation in the late nineteenth and early twentieth centuries. Most evolved from small individual operations, either ladies' tailors such as Vernon and Redfern, or dressmakers such as Madame Duboc and Barolet. Reville & Rossiter, on the other hand, began as a partnership between two former employees of a department store. All of them expanded during the late 1890s or the first decade of the twentieth century, supplying more expensive and formal clothing to an increasingly exclusive clientele. As London was a centre of fashion, almost all of Queen Maud's dress suppliers were situated there, although a few, like Madame Clapham, operated from towns close to her Appleton estate.

Madame Clapham aside, tracing the histories of most of these fashion houses is a challenge. Those that incorporated, such as Redfern and Reville & Rossiter, have related business records, but not all have survived in the Public Record Office in London. Some companies advertised regularly in leading fashion journals such as *The Queen* and *Vogue*, and their evolution can be traced through these sources. Others, such as Barolet and Blancquaert, did not advertise, presumably relying on word-of-mouth communication of their reputation. Determining the histories of these businesses is very difficult, with little to go by other than the London postal directories and an occasional description in a fashion journal.

Some companies, like Madame Duboc, were very short-lived, surviving for only a decade or so. Others, such as Redfern and Busvine, obviously spanned several generations of designers and directors, and managed to survive the vicissitudes of trade during the First World War, as well as adapting to the radical changes in fashion of the 1920s. The Depression was particularly hard on the fashion industry, and several companies survived by joining forces with the competition. Reville-Terry took over the London branch of Worth in 1936, at the same time as Busvine bought out Redfern.[2]

Cape, 1896

REDFERN, LONDON

The National Museum of Art/
Museum of Decorative Arts and Design, Oslo
OK 45-1962

328   THE QUEEN, THE LADY'S NEWSPAPER.   Aug. 1, 1896.

H.R.H. THE PRINCESS CHARLES OF DENMARK'S BLOUSES, CAPE, AND COSTUME, MADE BY MESSRS REDFERN, NEW BOND-STREET.

'HRH The Princess Charles of Denmark's blouses, cape and costume made by Messrs. Redfern, New Bond Street', *The Queen*, 1 August 1896

Queen Alexandra was a very good customer of Redfern, from whom she regularly purchased yachting ensembles and other sporting outfits throughout the 1880s and 1890s. She also bought yachting costumes, blouses, gowns and evening dresses for her three daughters, so it was natural for Redfern to be a significant supplier for Princess Maud's trousseau in 1896.

Only one item remains of the five gowns, several blouses and two capes that Redfern are credited with making for Princess Maud. An extract from *The Queen* describes in detail the company's contribution to the trousseau. Four day ensembles, two blouses and the cape were illustrated in two fashion plates published in the magazine with the following descriptions:

> *For her tailor-built gowns and capes Princess Maud went to Redfern, but that artist in costumes no longer confines himself to cloth and serge, but turns out the prettiest silk and other dresses that the heart of woman can desire ... Redfern is a past-master in blouses, and the Princess has a great many of them in the palest pink and blue chiné, in lilac scarcely darker than the tint of a cuckoo flower, in grass lawn and embroidery, and in striped batiste, with the daintiest lace-edged collars and cuffs imaginable ...*[3]

The cape, one of two in the trousseau, is described as follows: 'the other of fawn cloth, with a roll-over collar of Royal blue velvet, fanciful tabs of the same down the front and, at intervals, all round the edge'.[4]

Very few of the clothes featured in the vast numbers of fashion plates of this period survive. The cape provides an interesting example of the discrepancies between the fashion illustration and the real garment.

Walking suit, 1896

VERNON, LONDON

The National Museum of Art/
Museum of Decorative Arts and Design, Oslo
OK 73-1962

Although Redfern were one of the originators of the tailored walking suit in the 1870s, by the time of Maud's trousseau, every ladies' tailor in Britain was making this style of garment. Vernon made this walking suit for Princess Maud. Although not listed in the descriptions of her trousseau, it was said to have been worn on her honeymoon.[5] Several pre-1920 Vernon blouses, some elegantly feminine (page 71), and others shirt-style, as well as two sporty woollen dresses from the early 1920s, are to be found in Queen Maud's wardrobe (one is illustrated on page 67). Apart from the coronation dress (page 16) she did not seem to own any Vernon eveningwear, nor is Vernon mentioned in the dressers' notes.

The label in this suit describes Vernon as a 'tailor for ladies' and riding habits'. The company can be found in London Post Office directories listed as 'Vernon & Co. ladies tailors, habit makers and court dressmakers' from 1894 to 1924. It supplied clothes for Queen Alexandra, and was first listed with a Royal Warrant for Queen Maud in the 1914 directory. It must have had a reputation for being expensive, for a journalist writing in *The Ladies' Field* in 1911 recommended that readers visit Vernon and reassured them that it was untrue that only the very rich could purchase clothing there.[6]

According to an advert for Vernon in the same edition of the periodical, its specialities at this time were smart dresses for afternoon and evening use, sports clothing, elegant hats and blouses for any occasion. A special mention is made of its ability to cater for orders from abroad or out of town. Such orders were probably supplied by fitting on a bust made to a customer's measurements. This is probably how Vernon made clothes for Queen Maud, as one of her preserved dressmaker's mannequins is marked 'Vernon'.

Going-away dress, 1896

MADAME DUBOC, LONDON

The National Museum of Art/
Museum of Decorative Arts and Design, Oslo
OK 257-1991

After the wedding gown, the going-away dress was the next most important outfit in the trousseau. It was the first outfit that Princess Maud wore as a married woman, and carefully chosen so that she should be at her most beautiful for her husband. In addition, it had to appear smart and stylish to the crowds paying homage to the young couple as they travelled to their new home.

This ensemble consists of a dress with a matching cape in pink, one of Maud's favourite colours. It is a shot silk, with a strong pink warp and a light yellowish-green weft, producing a shimmering of colours as the fabric moves. The silhouette of the dress is typical of the 1890s, with a gored skirt flared at the back and a high-necked bodice with long, tight sleeves widening out into a puff at the top. The short cape has a wide border at the bottom made from cream-coloured lace and pink velvet decorated with black and silver beads, matching the decoration on the bodice.

Few details survive about the maker of the dress, Madame Leonie Duboc. She first appears in the London directories in 1895 as a court dressmaker, and her last entry is in 1907. A list of Royal Warrant Holders published in 1904 indicates that Madame Duboc was a dressmaker for Queen Alexandra as well.[7]

After the wedding, Princess Maud found it difficult to leave her family even though she would see them again in a few days. In a letter from Appleton House on 20 August, she describes what many brides must have felt: 'I had to keep back *all* my feelings as well as I could as there were *hundreds* of eyes looking! Real nightmare when I look back upon it.'[8]

Evening dress, *c.*1921

POSSIBLY BY BAROLET, LONDON

The National Museum of Art/
Museum of Decorative Arts and Design, Oslo
OK 215-1991

This evening gown may well be the one described in the dressers' notes as a 'silver-grey sequinned dress' worn at a hunt ball at Sandringham in January 1921 and at a dance at the palace in April. It is one of two sequinned dresses in Queen Maud's wardrobe that correspond to dresses by Barolet in the dressers' diaries (page 33). Both appear to be cut from one piece of material draped around the body, thus creating a relatively short skirt and a bodice without a marked waistline. They have square necklines, narrow shoulder straps, and short tulle sleeves.

This dress is embellished with long, silver-grey beads embroidered in a diamond pattern. The applied pink roses break the vertical lines of the dress, catching up the hem, a style very much in keeping with early 1920s fashions.

Like Maud's other 1920s evening dresses, this one has been shortened.

The first entry for this company in the London directories is 'Barolet, Felix (Madame), court dressmaker' in 1894. The last entry appears in 1927, 'Barolet, Felix, court dressmaker'. It obviously had exclusive clientele, as Felix Barolet is credited by the *London Illustrated News* with making the wedding dress of Queen Maud's niece Princess Alexandra, Duchess of Fife, in 1913, and described as a 'well-known Court Dressmaker'.[9] It is not certain when Maud first became its client, but a few outfits from Barolet are mentioned in the dressers' notes from 1919 to 1925. They include eveningwear, afternoon dresses, suits and outerwear.

Evening dress, *c.*1927

BLANCQUAERT, LONDON

The National Museum of Art/
Museum of Decorative Arts and Design, Oslo
OK 210-1991

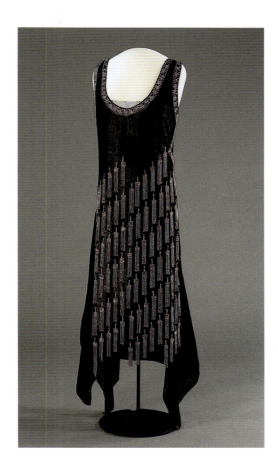

The evening dresses worn by Queen Maud during the last half of the 1920s were in considerable contrast to her earlier attire. In 1925–6, skirt lengths rose higher than ever, even for formal eveningwear. Young women wore knee-length skirts, and many older women raised their hemlines significantly in keeping with the new fashion. This dress, made from black chiffon with geometrically arranged decoration in diamanté, transparent and silver beads and sequins, is typical of the short evening fashions. Small tassels with long, beaded fringing are positioned in strict diagonal lines on the front of the skirt and in horizontal rows on the back. The dress is split at the side seams, with inserted gores of chiffon ending in points below the hemline of the dress. The insertions and the embroidered tassels would have come to life at the slightest movement.

A long train decorated with matching tassels and lined with silver lamé belongs to the dress. The train, which attached at the shoulder seams, indicates that the dress must have been made for formal occasions. It was probably first worn at the annual dinner for Members of Parliament in January 1927.

John Blancquaert first appears in the London directories as a ladies' tailor in 1903. From 1928, the company was listed as 'Mme. & M. Blancquaert, court dressmaker and ladies' tailors' until it closed in 1941. The firm made high-profile clothing, as descriptions in magazines such as *The Ladies' Field* affirm.[10] Queen Maud's patronage of Blancquaert probably started in the 1920s, as its outfits are mentioned in the dressers' notes between 1924 and 1938. The entries in the directories suggest a family business, and the labels in Queen Maud's dresses are variously marked 'J. Blancquaert & Co', 'B. Blancquaert & Co' and 'M.sieur et M.dme Blancquaert'.

Afternoon dress, 1933

BLANCQUAERT, LONDON

The National Museum of Art/
Museum of Decorative Arts and Design, Oslo
OK 97-1991

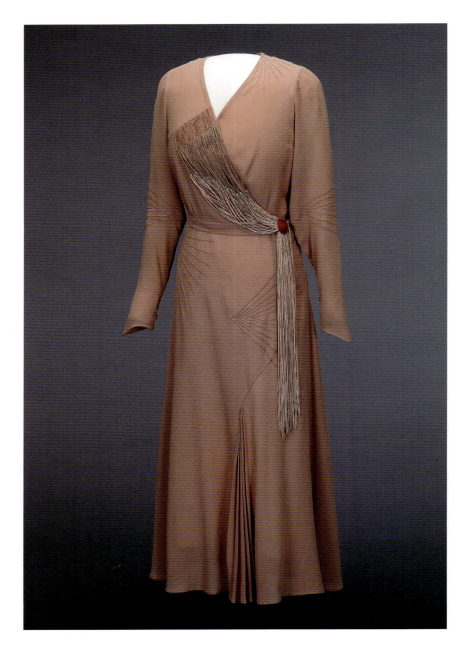

Queen Maud wore this beige silk dress in 1933 for Queen Mary's birthday, and at a tea dance in the British legation in Oslo. It has a large, orange-red button and eye-catching silk cords in two shades of beige. The cords cross the bodice diagonally; there they are held by the button at the left side and fall from the waist. A pleated gore at the hemline and decorative pin-tucks sewn in fan shapes at the shoulder, sleeve and hip illustrate the high degree of dressmaking skill exhibited by the maker Blancquaert.

The company was also expert at tailored suits and made at least one for Queen Maud, which is illustrated on page 58, as well as the coat for winter sports shown on page 68.

Day dress, 1930–35

BLANCQUAERT, LONDON

The National Museum of Art/
Museum of Decorative Arts and Design, Oslo
OK 100-1991

This is another example of excellent couture detail by Blancquaert. The dress is very plain, in a simple shift style with long sleeves and belted at the waist. The rich shade of purple of the dress is enhanced by intricate pin-tucking in the shape of leaves on the bodice and sleeves. The leaf forms carry over into a draped trim at the left front, lined in contrasting fuschia silk. Mirroring this fall of fabric is the tie of the belt. This and the other garments by Blancquaert in Queen Maud's wardrobe illustrate the relaxed elegance emphasized by exciting cut and details that characterize the company's production. They demonstrate that the less-known fashion houses, many of which are nearly forgotten today, maintained a high quality in terms of both sewing and design.

Evening dress, 1937

BLANCQUAERT, LONDON

The National Museum of Art/
Museum of Decorative Arts and Design, Oslo
OK 25-1962

104 This elegant blue and silver brocade evening dress is characteristic of the styles of the late 1930s and also of Queen Maud's preference for a slender profile. The cut of the gown is very simple in order to enhance the splendid design of the silk. A V-shaped panel dominates the front like an eighteenth-century stomacher. At each side of it, the fabric is gathered, allowing it to drape elegantly around the back.

By the late 1930s, a train indicated a very formal event.

The dress was worn for a banquet held during the coronation ceremonies of George VI in 1937. The queen was dressed in Blancquaert clothing for several major events. In addition to the garments illustrated here, the company supplied the beaded, beige and gold lace evening gown worn during the wedding celebrations for her son in 1929 (page 36), and a dress coat that she wore in the cathedral during the Norwegian Silver Jubilee in 1930.

Norwegian Designers

When Queen Maud came to Norway in 1905, there were high hopes that she would patronize the leading fashion houses in Norway. The disappointment was correspondingly great when it transpired that Maud had no plans to dress in Norwegian clothing. She was thirty-six years old when she arrived in Norway, so it was perhaps understandable that she remained loyal to the British and French companies that had supplied her clothing for at least a decade and with whom she had developed good business relationships. In the small society of Kristiania (Oslo), she may also have found it difficult to favour some fashion companies over others. However, when she did shop in Kristiania, it was for specialist clothing such as ski-wear and sports furs, and to support the business of a close friend. She may have also relied on local suppliers at times when it was impossible to get the clothing she needed from England, for example during the First World War.

Queen Maud's contact with Silkehuset regarding the coronation gown (page 16) must have started just after she arrived in Norway, probably on the recommendation of people connected with the court. Silkehuset was founded in 1897. One of the founders, Rolf Halvorsen, took over the company shortly afterwards, and under his direction it became one of the leading companies in the silk trade and later developed a couture and fur department. Silkehuset was well prepared for a great rush of customers who required elegant dresses for the coronation celebrations in Trondhjem. On 1 May 1906, it placed an advert in the newspaper *Morgenbladet* with the headline 'The Coronation in Trondhjem'. Potential customers were informed that they could buy their *Robes de Cérémonie*, *Robes de Cour* and *Robes de Bal* from Silkehuset, all in the latest fashion purchased in Paris, London and Brussels.

The only piece of hard evidence linking Silkehuset and the coronation gown is the sample of embroidery that for many years was exhibited at Silkehuset. The sample is clearly a tester, where several ideas have been tried, for the pattern drawn differs somewhat from that seen on the dress. There could be many reasons why Silkehuset's contact with Queen Maud ceased after the coronation dress was supplied. Perhaps it emphasized its role in the gown more than she would have liked? Silkehuset would have been well able to continue making clothes for Maud had she chosen to patronize Norwegian fashion houses.

After the death of Rolf Halvorsen in 1926, his nephew Rolf Grieg-Halvorsen became the sole owner. He took over running of the couture department, which soon became one of the principal fashion outlets in Norway. In an advertisement placed in the periodical *Vi Selv og våre hjem* (Ourselves and our home) in April 1934, Silkehuset reported that it concentrated on acquiring good, signed designer models and that the following fashion houses were represented by it: Augustabernard, Barton, Lanvin, Lelong, Mainbocher, Molyneux, Patou, Raphael, Rochas, Vionnet and Schiaparelli. The success of the couture department continued until the late 1950s under the leadership of the Grieg-Halvorsen family. The company changed hands in 1960, and ceased trading in 1974.[1]

Queen Maud also acquired other specialist garments from Norwegian companies, like ski-wear from the ladies' tailor Frode Braathen in the early 1930s (page 69). A fur jacket that she wears in many photographs from Voksenkollen in December 1905 is labelled 'P. Backer, furriers'. The company was founded in 1856 by Johan Paul Jørgen Alexander Backer. By the end of the 1870s, it had become a specialist supplier of furs and remained in business until 1980. From 1895, the company annually issued an illustrated catalogue of its goods in four languages, and until the First World War, it took part in several exhibitions both at home and abroad.

Gina Andersen Moen is said to have supplied clothing to the queen for a period.[2] She was born in Ullensaker but went to Kristiania, where she trained as a seamstress. In 1885, she opened her own business, which became one of the top dressmaking establishments in Kristiania, employing about eighty seamstresses at the height of its success. Her career paralleled that of Madame Clapham in some respects, and the quality of her clothes equalled that of British and French fashion houses. Gina Andersen Moen retired in 1920; unfortunately, nothing she made for Queen Maud has been identified in the wardrobe.

Sylvian was probably the only fashion house in Oslo where Queen Maud made regular purchases for the duration of the business. The reason was her friendship with the owner, Sylvia Schou, who made the acquaintance of the queen around 1912. Sylvia's husband lost his fortune after the First World War and she began a dressmaking business, named Sylvian, to support her family. When Queen Maud became a client with Sylvian, it was probably to help a friend in a difficult situation.

Every spring and autumn, Sylvia Schou visited Paris to update herself on fashion and to purchase sample dresses from different fashion houses. These were then copied at Sylvian's workshop. Some of the outfits sold by Sylvian were designed in Norway, possibly by the French painter Hélène Perdriat, who was Sylvia's sister-in-law. Queen Maud mainly had afternoon outfits made by Sylvian, but also some more formal dresses. Sylvian ceased trading in 1935.[3]

Evening dress, 1924–5

SYLVIAN, OSLO

The National Museum of Art/
Museum of Decorative Arts and Design, Oslo
OK 186-1991

This is one of only two garments in Queen Maud's wardrobe that can be identified as made by Sylvian. The simple shape of the dress is similar to that of other evening gowns of the mid-1920s in Queen Maud's wardrobe. It is made of copper-coloured fabric, decorated with floral embroidery in bold colours, and edged with fur at the hem. The flowers are cut from a floral patterned cotton fabric and are appliquéd with shiny silk thread and matt chenille yarn. Ida Hellesen, Sylvia Schou's mother, was an expert in this type of appliqué embroidery, and several similar pieces have been preserved, suggesting that she may have worked this dress as well.

108

Jacket, *c.*1925

SYLVIAN, OSLO

The National Museum of Art/
Museum of Decorative Arts and Design, Oslo
OK 268-1991

Another example of Sylvian's production for Queen Maud is this jacket covered in woollen embroidery in an orientally inspired design. Animals, birds and flowers in orange, rust, black and white enliven what is otherwise a very simple garment. The embroidery is executed in coarse wool and is most effective.

NOTES

INTRODUCTION
1. Anne Kjellberg, *Dronning Maud*, Oslo, Grøndahl og Dreyers Forlag, 1995 p. 6
2. Valerie Cumming, *Royal Dress*, London, Batsford, 1989, p. 158

BIOGRAPHY
1. Sandra Barwick, *A Century of Style*, London, George Allen & Unwin, 1984, p. 5
2. Kjellberg, p. 14
3. *The Queen*, 25 July 1896, p. 160 and 1 August 1896, p. 219
4. Website: www.odin.dep.no

ROYAL ROBES
1. Princess Maud to Mary, Princess of Wales, 17 December 1905, Royal Archives, G.V. CC. 45/285
2. Ibid., 22 March 1906, RA G.V. CC. 45/289
3. Queen Maud to Queen Mary, 20 May 1937, RA G.V. CC. 45/1100g
4. Catherine Join-Diéterle, ed., *Femmes fin de siècle 1885–1895*, Musée de la Mode et du Costume, Paris, 1990, p. 188
5. Ibid.
6. Letter from Françoise Vittu to Anne Kjellberg, 13 October 1993
7. Interview Anne Kjellberg with Rolf Grieg-Halvorsen Jr., former head of the couture department at Silkehuset, 5 May 1992
8. *The Sphere*, 30 June 1906, p. 282
9. *Morgenbladet*, 15 June 1905 and *Trondhjems Adresseavis*, 16 June 1906
10. Una Campbell, *Robes of the Realm. 300 Years of Ceremonial Dress*, London, Michael O'Mara Books Ltd., 1989, pp. 27–41
11. Ede and Ravenscroft Ltd. Ledger (1902). MS 21.694, Vol. H., I

EVENING DRESS
1. *Urd*, 9 December 1905
2. Interview Anne Kjellberg with Sylvia Wiese, daughter of the owner of Sylvian, a Norwegian fashion firm patronized by Queen Maud, 12 June 1992
3. *Morgenbladet*, 23 June 1906
4. *Femina*, 1 June 1907, p. 238
5. Queen Maud to Mary, Princess of Wales, 23 May 1907, RA, GV. CC. 45/303
6. *The Lady's Realm*, May 1906, p. 114
7. Queen Maud to Queen Mary, 18 February 1920, RA G.V. CC. 45/582
8. Interview Anne Kjellberg with Violet Wond, the Queen's last dresser, 1 July 1993

DAYWEAR
1. *Haakon VII – Dronning Maud*, Kristiania, Narvesens Kioskkompagni, 1905

2. Interview Anne Kjellberg with Violet Wond, the Queen's last dresser, 1 July 1993
3. Queen Maud to Queen Mary, 30 March 1935, RA G.V. CC 45/956
4. Amy de la Haye, ed., *The Cutting Edge: 50 Years of British Fashion 1947–1997*, London, V&A Museum, pp. 50–1
5. Georgina O'Hara Callan, *Dictionary of Fashion and Fashion Designers*, London, Thames & Hudson, 1998, p. 200 and Public Record Office, London, BT/17615/86706
6. Callan, p. 200
7. PRO, BT/17615/86706/30, 9 August 1912 and BT/17615/86706/32, 30 December 1912
8. PRO, BT/17615/86706/34, 13 June 1919
9. *Vogue* UK, Early November 1924, p. iii
10. PRO, BT/35684/313974/6, 28 May 1936
11. *Vogue* UK, 19 September 1934, p. 21 and 20 March 1935, p. 21
12. *The Times*, 9 October 1948, p. 6

SPORTSWEAR
1. Princess Maud to Mary, Princess of Wales, 22 March 1906, RA G.V. CC. 45/289
2. *The Queen*, 25 July 1896, p. 160
3. Ibid., p. 161
4. Thelma H. Benjamin, *London Shops & Shopping*, London, 1934, p. 97
5. Garnier, Guillaume, ed., *Paris-Couture-Année Trente*. Paris: Editions Paris-Musées et Société de l'Histoire de Costume, 1987, p. 243 and *Vogue* UK, 9 November 1932, p. 5 and 11 November 1936 p. 47
6. *Urd*, December 1934, p. 1373f

ACCESSORIES
1. *The Queen*, 25 July 1896, p. 161
2. Queen Maud to Queen Mary, 28 December 1926, RA G.V. CC. 45/703
3. Georgina Battiscombe, *Queen Alexandra*, London, Constable, 1969, p. 203
4. Jayne Tyler and Clare Parsons, *Madame Clapham. Hull's celebrated dressmaker*, Kingston upon Hull, Kingston upon Hull City Museums and Art Galleries, 1999, p. 10
5. Ann Crowther, *Madame Clapham. The Celebrated Dressmaker*, City of Kingston upon Hull Museums & Art Galleries, 1977
6. Ibid.
7. Tyler and Parsons, p. 3
8. Ibid., p. 9
9. Ibid., p. 5
10. Ibid., p. 3
11. Ibid., p. 7
12. Ibid., chapters 5 and 6, pp. 15–22
13. Ibid., p. 24

DESIGNERS – FRENCH
1. Queen Maud to Queen Mary, 25 September 1923, RA G.V. CC. 45/627
2. Letter from Toni Julius, director of Gems Ltd., formerly The French Bust Company, to the Museum of Decorative Arts and Design, Oslo, 25 November 1992
3. Coleman, Elizabeth Ann, *The Opulent Era: Fashion of Worth, Doucet and Pingat*, London and Brooklyn, Thames & Hudson and the Brooklyn Museum, 1990, p. 98, p. 95f,
4. Kjellberg, p. 115
5. Letter from Jean de Moüy, director of Patou, to the Museum of Decorative Arts and Design, Oslo, 20 July 1994
6. *The Queen*, 10 July 1897, p. 73
7. Ibid., p. 73
8. *Morgenbladet*, 26 June 1906
9. *L'Art et la Mode*, 8 June 1907, p. 491
10. Kjellberg, p. 110
11. Katia Johansen, *Kongelige Kjoler*, København, Rosenborg, 1990, p. 17
12. *L'Art et la Mode*, 24 October 1885, p. 558

13. *The Queen*,13 June 1896, p.1066 and 25 July 1896, p. 196
14. Barwick, p. 92 and Battiscombe, p. 218f
15. Jean Philippe Worth, *A Century of Fashion*, Boston: Little, Brown and Company, 1928, p. 181
16. Coleman, p. 21
17. *The Queen*, 14 October 1911, p. 687
18. Coleman, p. 23
19. *Vogue* UK, 19 August 1936, p. 46
20. Coleman, p. 23

DESIGNERS – BRITISH
1. Barwick, p. 22 and Diana de Marly, *The History of Haute Couture*, London, Batsford, 1986, pp. 59–62
2. *Vogue* UK, 19 August 1936, p. 46
3. *The Queen*, 25 July 1896, p. 160
4. Ibid.
5. Written on a piece of paper attached to the suit when it came to the Museum of Decorative Arts and Design, Oslo: 'Tweed outfit worn on honeymoon'.
6. *The Ladies' Field*, 9 December 1911, the page is unnumbered and inserted between XXXVIII and XLI (sic). The advert is on p. 21
7. *List of Royal Warrant Holders*, London: Royal Warrant Holders Association, 1904, p. 49
8. Princess Maud to Mary, Duchess of York, 20 August 1896, RA G.V. CC. 45/173
9. *London Illustrated News*, 18 October 1913, pp. 628 and 629
10. *The Ladies' Field*, 23 March 1912, 'Gowns Worn at Their Majesties' Court'

DESIGNERS – NORWEGIAN
1. Interview Anne Kjellberg with Rolf Grieg-Halvorsen Jr., former head of the couture department at Silkehuset, 5 May 1992; letter from Ivar Eriksen, former office manager at Silkehuset, 27 October 1975, in the Archives of the National Museum of Art/Museum of Decorative Arts and Design, Oslo.
2. Interview Anne Kjellberg with Wilhelmine Romsås, niece of Gina Andersen Moen,1994. Cutting from unknown newspaper, May 1937
3. Interview Anne Kjellberg with Sylvia Wiese, daughter of the owner of Sylvian, 12 June 1992

GLOSSARY

DIAMANTÉ – a colourless glass paste used for decorating costume jewellery and for applying to dress fabrics (often sold in strips ready for sewing).

FROG – an ornamental fastening of knotted braid or fabric

LAMÉ – a fabric woven with narrow strips of metal thread

PRINCESS STYLE – a style of construction where a dress is cut in one piece without a waist seam. It usually features a close-fitting bodice which expands to a full skirt below the waist. The princess style was intermittently fashionable from the 1860s through to the late 1930s.

STRAPWORK – ornament consisting of interlaced bands

SELECT BIBLIOGRAPHY

Adburgham, Alice, *Shops and Shopping 1800–1914*, London: George Allen & Unwin, 1964

Arch, Nigel and Joanna Marschner, *Splendour at Court: Dressing for Royal Occasions since 1700*, London: Unwin Hyman, 1987

————, *The Royal Wedding Dresses*, London: Sidgwick & Jackson, 1990

Barwick, Sandra, *A Century of Style*, London, George Allen & Unwin, 1984

Byrde, Penelope, *A Visual History of Costume: The Twentieth Century*, London: Batsford, 1987

Campbell, Una, *Robes of the Realm. 300 Years of Ceremonial Dress*, London, Michael O'Mara Books Ltd., 1989

Cumming, Valerie, *Royal Dress*, London: Batsford, 1989

de Marly, Diana, *The History of Haute Couture 1850–1950*, London: Batsford, 1980

Deslandres, Yvonne, and Françoise Muller, *Histoire de la Mode au XXe Siecle*, Paris: Somogy, 1986

Ewing, Elizabeth, *History of Twentieth Century Fashion*, London: Batsford, 1974

Four Hundred Years of Fashion, London: V&A, 1992

Garnier, Guillaume, ed., *Paris-Couture-Année Trente*. Paris: Editions Paris-Musées et Société de l'Histoire de Costume, 1987

Gernsheim, Alison, *Victorian and Edwardian Fashion. A Photographic Survey*, New York: Dover, 1981

Ginsburg, Madeleine, ed., *Fashion: an Anthology by Cecil Beaton*, London: HMSO, 1971

Join-Diéterle, Catherine, ed., *Femmes fin de siècle 1885–1895*, Musée de la Mode et du Costume, Paris, 1990

————, ed., *Robes du soir 1850–1990*, Musée de la Mode et du Costume, Paris, 1990

Levitt, Sarah, *Fashion in Photographs, 1880–1900*, London: Batsford and the National Portrait Gallery, 1991

Lussier, Suzanne, *Art Deco Fashion*, London: V&A, 2003

McDowell, Colin, *McDowell's Directory of Twentieth Century Fashion*, London: Frederick Muller, 1984

Mendes, Valerie and Amy de la Haye, *20th Century Fashion*, London: Thames & Hudson, 1999

Millbank, Caroline, R., *Couture: The Great Fashion Designers*, London: Thames & Hudson, 1985

Mulvagh, Jane, *Vogue History of 20th Century Fashion*, London: Viking, 1988

Murphy, Sophia, *The Duchess of Devonshire's Ball*, London: Sidgwick & Jackson, 1984

Roley, Katrina and Caroline Aish, *Fashion in Photographs 1900–1920*, London: Batsford and the National Portrait Gallery, 1992

Tyler, Jayne and Clare Parsons, *Madame Clapham. Hull's*

111

Celebrated Dressmaker, Kingston upon Hull: Kingston upon Hull City Museums and Art Galleries, 1999

Walkley, Christine, *Dressed to Impress: 1840–1914*, London: Batsford, 1989

Wilson, Elizabeth and Lou Taylor, *Through the Looking Glass*, London: BBC Books, 1989

DESIGNERS

Blum, Dilys, *Shocking Schiaparelli*, Philadelphia: Philadelphia Museum of Art, 2003

Callan, Georgina O'Hara, *Dictionary of Fashion and Fashion Designers*, London, Thames & Hudson, 1998

Coleman, Elizabeth Ann, *The Opulent Era: Fashion of Worth, Doucet and Pingat*, London and Brooklyn: Thames & Hudson and the Brooklyn Museum, 1990

de la Haye, Amy and Shelley Tobin, *Chanel: The Couturiere at Work*, London: V&A, 1994

de Marly, Diana, *Worth: Father of Haute Couture*, London: Elm Tree Books, 1980

de Osma, Guillermo, *Mariano Fortuny: His Life and Work*, New York: Rizzoli, 1980

Mackrell, Alice, *Coco Chanel*, London: Batsford, 1992

———————, *Paul Poiret*, London: Batsford, 1990

Worth, Jean Philippe, *A Century of Fashion*, Boston: Little, Brown and Company, 1928

112

INDEX OF DESIGNER/MAKERS FOR QUEEN MAUD
(page numbers in bold indicate biographical details)